# The Tapestry of Life

# The Tapestry of Life

## God's Grace in the Midst of Suffering

PATRICK O'DONNELL

XULON PRESS

Xulon Press
555 Winderley Pl, Suite 225
Maitland, FL 32751
407.339.4217
www.xulonpress.com

© 2024 by Patrick O'Donnell

All rights reserved solely by the author. The author guarantees all contents are original and do not infringe upon the legal rights of any other person or work. No part of this book may be reproduced in any form without the permission of the author.

Due to the changing nature of the Internet, if there are any web addresses, links, or URLs included in this manuscript, these may have been altered and may no longer be accessible. The views and opinions shared in this book belong solely to the author and do not necessarily reflect those of the publisher. The publisher therefore disclaims responsibility for the views or opinions expressed within the work.

Unless otherwise indicated, Scripture quotations taken from the Holy Bible, New International Version (NIV). Copyright © 1973, 1978, 1984, 2011 by Biblica, Inc.™. Used by permission. All rights reserved.

Paperback ISBN-13: 979-8-86850-289-7
Ebook ISBN-13: 979-8-86850-290-3

# Contents

Dedication . . . . . . . . . . . . . . . . . . . . . . . . . . . . . . . . . xi
Introduction . . . . . . . . . . . . . . . . . . . . . . . . . . . . . . . xiii

The Journey of Healing . . . . . . . . . . . . . . . . . . . . . . . . . 1
A Ministry of Wounded Hearts . . . . . . . . . . . . . . . . . . . 3
Anxiety is a Thief . . . . . . . . . . . . . . . . . . . . . . . . . . . . . 5
Embrace Your Brokenness . . . . . . . . . . . . . . . . . . . . . . 7
The Treasure of People . . . . . . . . . . . . . . . . . . . . . . . . . 9
The Gift of Humility . . . . . . . . . . . . . . . . . . . . . . . . . 11
Ministering to Suffering Souls . . . . . . . . . . . . . . . . . . 13
Love is Serving One Another . . . . . . . . . . . . . . . . . . . 15
The Precious Gift of Life . . . . . . . . . . . . . . . . . . . . . . 19
You Matter! . . . . . . . . . . . . . . . . . . . . . . . . . . . . . . . . 21
Walking in Gratitude . . . . . . . . . . . . . . . . . . . . . . . . . 23
Embracing the Outsider: Love Over Judgment . . . . . . 25
Become Who You Are . . . . . . . . . . . . . . . . . . . . . . . . 27
The Difference Between Guilt and Shame . . . . . . . . . . 29
Hearing the Voice of God . . . . . . . . . . . . . . . . . . . . . 31
Compassion Fatigue . . . . . . . . . . . . . . . . . . . . . . . . . 33
The Courage of Vulnerability . . . . . . . . . . . . . . . . . . 35
Silent Suffering . . . . . . . . . . . . . . . . . . . . . . . . . . . . . 37
Resting in God . . . . . . . . . . . . . . . . . . . . . . . . . . . . . 41
Who Defines You? . . . . . . . . . . . . . . . . . . . . . . . . . . 43

| | |
|---|---|
| Grappling with Doubt | 45 |
| The Crucible of Suffering | 47 |
| Cultivating Humility | 49 |
| Embracing our Brokenness | 51 |
| Becoming Stuck in Grief | 53 |
| Recapturing the Rhythm of Life | 57 |
| The Onslaught of Abuse | 59 |
| Connections | 63 |
| Hope, Faith, and Love | 65 |
| Practicing Gentleness | 67 |
| Wounded by Words | 69 |
| We are Revelators of God | 71 |
| The Solace of Silent Ministry | 73 |
| Beautiful People | 75 |
| Bumping into Absences | 77 |
| Journeying Through the Darkness | 79 |
| Tending to Our Souls | 81 |
| Battered by Betrayal | 83 |
| Work as Worship | 85 |
| The Wilderness of Uncertainty | 87 |
| Overcoming Obstacles to Growth | 89 |
| God: Our Dwelling Place | 91 |
| Hope for Healing | 93 |
| The Pain of Being Misunderstood | 95 |
| God's Whispers in the Wind | 99 |
| Moments of Wonder | 101 |
| Living with Eternity in View | 103 |
| Gratitude for Scars | 105 |
| The Gift of Time | 107 |
| The Challenge of Belief | 109 |

| | |
|---|---|
| God's Comfort for Weary Souls | 113 |
| Navigating Disappointment with Grace | 115 |
| Waiting in the Midst of the Storm | 117 |
| The Transformative Love of God | 119 |
| Divine Interruptions | 123 |
| The Whirlwind of the Unknown | 125 |
| Spiritual Fingerprints | 127 |
| Providing Sanctuary | 129 |
| A Lifetime of Friends | 131 |
| Navigating the Storms of Life | 133 |
| Liminal Spaces | 135 |
| In the Shadow of Betrayal | 137 |
| Fellow Pilgrims in the Journey of Life | 139 |
| The Nearness of God | 141 |
| The Sacred Dance of Everyday Existence | 143 |
| When Life Doesn't Make Sense | 145 |
| Threads of Frailty and Fragility | 147 |
| When the Wheels Come Off | 149 |
| Navigating the Beauty and Ugliness of Existence | 151 |
| When Hope Feels Like a Four-Letter Word | 153 |
| The Blessing of Adversity | 155 |
| Feeling Stuck | 157 |
| Developing Resilience | 159 |
| Is Love Enough? | 161 |
| Reconciliation | 165 |
| You are Enough! | 167 |
| Worthy of Love | 169 |
| Cultivating Hope | 171 |
| The Wilderness of Suffering | 173 |
| The Inner Sanctum of Our Souls | 175 |

| | |
|---|---|
| Interludes of Vulnerability | 177 |
| The Sacred Space of Accountability | 179 |
| Infusing Joy | 181 |
| Radical Acceptance | 183 |
| Facing Unjust Treatment | 185 |
| Embracing our Uniqueness | 187 |
| Yearning for Connection | 189 |
| True Beauty | 191 |
| The Call to Love Radically | 193 |
| Holy Inefficiency | 197 |
| The Journey Through Suffering | 199 |
| Moments of Grandeur | 201 |
| Embrace the Cross | 203 |
| The Depths of Desolation | 205 |
| The Wounds of Betrayal | 207 |
| The Privilege of Old Age | 211 |
| Lights in the Darkness | 213 |
| Fighting for Joy | 215 |
| The Sufficiency of God | 217 |
| Living from a Grace-Based Perspective | 219 |
| The Sacred Act of Listening | 221 |
| The Simplest Form of Gratitude | 223 |
| A Grace-Led Life | 225 |
| Committing No Errors and Still Losing | 227 |
| The Miracle of a Moment | 231 |
| Relinquishing the Right to be Right | 233 |
| Trusting God in Difficulty | 235 |
| The Battle for Joy | 237 |
| Willing the Will of God After Him | 241 |
| "I'm Too Busy" | 243 |

| | |
|---|---|
| The Art of Being | 245 |
| Living as a Forgiven Person | 247 |
| Sweet Dreams | 249 |
| Forgive Again | 251 |
| Seasons of Darkness | 253 |
| A Fresh Thought from God | 255 |
| The Apprenticeship of Adversity | 259 |
| The Fingerprints of God | 261 |
| Seasons of Waiting | 265 |
| The Expanse of God's Grace | 267 |
| The Singular Gift of a Day | 271 |
| The Pursuit of Wisdom | 273 |
| When the Path Ahead is Not Clear | 275 |
| Keeping in Step with the Spirit of God | 279 |
| Goodness: A Fruit of the Spirit | 283 |
| The Sacred Act of Listening | 287 |
| The Extraordinary Gift of Life | 289 |
| The Courageous Journey of Reconciliation | 291 |
| Peace and Patience: Sibling Fruits of the Spirit | 293 |
| The Beauty of Uncertainty | 295 |
| Gratitude in the Midst of Suffering | 297 |
| Jehoshaphat's Prayer | 299 |
| Finding Hope in the Midst of Despair | 303 |
| Living with Chronic Pain | 307 |
| Bibliography | 311 |

# DEDICATION

*"To my family and friends, and especially to my wife, Barbara. Thank you for sharing the journey with me."*

*"A special thanks to Kathy Stagg Ward who graciously served as a reader."*

# INTRODUCTION

Life is often compared to a tapestry—a beautiful, intricate weave of threads that, when viewed up close, may appear chaotic and disordered. But when we step back and observe the broader picture, we see a masterpiece of divine design. This collection of devotionals explores the threads that make up the tapestry of life, each devotional a reflection on the different colors, textures, and patterns that come together to form the fabric of our existence.

In quiet moments of reflection and prayer, we often find ourselves contemplating the various experiences that have shaped us. Some of these experiences are joyful; filled with vibrant hues that bring warmth to our hearts. Others are marked by sorrow and pain; darker threads that add depth and contrast to the overall picture. Yet, it is the combination of these elements—the light and the dark; the smooth and the rough—that create a rich and meaningful tapestry.

One of the most profound aspects of the tapestry of life is the interplay between pain and joy. These two seemingly opposing forces are, in reality, deeply intertwined. It is through our experiences of pain that we often come to appreciate the moments of joy more fully. In the devotionals included in this book, you will find reflections on the nature of suffering, the ways in which it can lead to spiritual growth, and a deeper understanding of God's grace.

Living with chronic pain, for example, can feel like carrying a heavy burden each day. Yet, within this struggle lies the potential for resilience and strength. The devotional on chronic pain explores how this experience can become a crucible for refining our faith and developing empathy for others. It reminds us that strength is not always about overcoming pain but about finding the courage to face each day despite it.

On the other hand, moments of joy, no matter how fleeting, offer glimpses of God's goodness and love. They are like the bright, colorful threads that stand out against the darker background, illuminating the beauty of the tapestry. These moments remind us to give thanks and to savor the blessings that come our way, even amidst life's challenges.

Another essential theme in the tapestry of life is the role of relationships. The people we encounter, the bonds we form, and the love we share all contribute to the richness of our lives. Each relationship adds a unique thread to the tapestry, creating intricate patterns that reflect our connections with others.

The devotionals in this collection delve into the complexities of relationships, from the joy of companionship to the heartache of loss. They explore the ways in which our interactions with others can shape our spiritual journey. For instance, the devotional on the absence left behind when a loved one dies addresses the profound impact of grief. It acknowledges the void that loss creates and offers a compassionate perspective on finding hope and healing in the aftermath.

Similarly, the devotional on silent suffering emphasizes the importance of empathy and understanding. It speaks to the quiet battles that many people face and encourages us to reach out with kindness and support. These reflections remind us that we are not alone in our struggles and that our relationships can be a source of strength and comfort.

In our fast-paced world, it is easy to become consumed by the demands of daily life and lose sight of the present moment. The devotionals in this collection invite us to slow down and to savor the beauty of simply being. They encourage us to cultivate mindfulness and to appreciate the gifts that each day brings.

# Introduction

As you journey through the devotionals in this book, may you find inspiration, comfort, and hope. Each reflection is a thread in the tapestry of life, contributing to the overall picture of God's grace and love. Whether you are facing moments of joy or seasons of pain, may these devotionals remind you that you are part of a greater design, woven together with purpose and care.

Life's tapestry is ever evolving, shaped by our experiences, relationships, and spiritual growth. It is a testament to the resilience of the human spirit and the enduring power of faith. As you navigate the threads of your own life, may you discover the beauty in both the light and dark, and may you find strength in the knowledge that you are never alone.

In the pages that follow, let us embark on a journey of reflection and discovery, exploring the myriad ways in which God's grace is woven into the fabric of our lives. May this book be a source of encouragement and a reminder of the intricate and beautiful tapestry that is our life in Christ.

## The Grand Design of Life

In the intricate weaving of life, we are each a tapestry, composed of countless threads. The richness of our experiences, joys, sorrows, triumphs, and challenges all interlace to create a unique and beautiful masterpiece.

Like a tapestry, our lives often reveal their beauty when viewed from a distance. In the midst of chaos and hardship, it's easy to focus on the individual threads – moments of pain, confusion, or struggle. But stepping back allows us to appreciate the grand design being formed, the patterns that emerge, and the story being woven.

Sometimes, it's the darker threads, the difficult times, that give depth and contrast to the overall picture. They're integral to the beauty of the final piece. Just as in life, our trials and hardships can ultimately contribute to our growth, resilience, and empathy;

## The Tapestry of Life

each thread represents a moment, an encounter, a decision, or a circumstance. Some threads may shine brilliantly, while others might seem dull or frayed. Yet, when all these threads are skillfully woven together, they form a coherent and intricate narrative of our existence.

Our lives as tapestries remind us of the Master Weaver—whether seen or unseen—skillfully crafting each moment, choosing every thread, and expertly blending contrasting shades. It speaks of intentionality and purpose behind every twist and turn.

Embracing our lives as tapestries allows us to find beauty in the imperfections, appreciate the complexity of our experiences, and trust that there's a grand design unfolding. Every thread matters, and every part of our story contributes to the masterpiece that is our lives. When we look closely at a tapestry, we see individual threads; each with its own unique color and texture. Some threads are vibrant and eye-catching, representing our moments of joy and triumph. These are the moments that make our hearts sing and our spirits soar. They are the bright spots in our lives, reminding us of the goodness and beauty that exist in the world.

Other threads, however, are dark and muted, representing our times of sorrow and hardship. These are the moments that test our faith and challenge our resilience. They are the times when we feel lost and alone, struggling to find our way. But these dark threads are just as important as the bright ones. They give our lives depth and complexity, adding contrast and richness to the overall tapestry.

It's often the darker threads that allow the brighter ones to shine even more brilliantly. In the same way, our struggles and hardships can highlight the beauty and goodness in our lives, making our moments of joy and triumph even more meaningful. Without the dark threads, the tapestry of our lives would be flat and one-dimensional. It's the contrast between the light and dark threads that creates a dynamic and engaging narrative.

# INTRODUCTION

As we navigate through life, we may not always see the grand design that is being woven. We may question the purpose of certain threads, wondering why we have to endure pain and suffering. But just as a tapestry reveals its full beauty when viewed from a distance, so too does our life reveal its true purpose and meaning when we step back and see the bigger picture.

The Master Weaver, whether we recognize Him or not, is always at work, skillfully blending the threads of our lives into a cohesive and beautiful masterpiece. He knows which threads to use and when to use them, weaving them together with intentionality and purpose. He takes the seemingly random and chaotic moments of our lives and arranges them into a pattern that is both intricate and meaningful.

When we embrace our lives as tapestries, we learn to trust in the Master Weaver's plan. We come to understand that every thread, no matter how dark or frayed, has a place in the overall design. We find beauty in the imperfections and appreciate the complexity of our experiences. We recognize that every part of our story, no matter how small or insignificant it may seem, contributes to the masterpiece that is our lives.

So, the next time you find yourself caught in the midst of chaos and hardship, remember the tapestry. Take a step back and see the bigger picture. Trust that the Master Weaver is at work, weaving each thread with care and intention. Embrace the beauty of your life, with all its twists and turns, and know that you are a unique and beautiful masterpiece, crafted with love and purpose.

# The Journey of Healing

Healing is not a linear process. It takes mind, body, and soul to explore who we were and who we are. It is not a battle but instead an opportunity to tend to our wounds. Reflecting on the causes, acknowledging how we feel, and then seeing where we are in the present gives us the capacity for joy while we tend to the hurt.

There are present moments that pull us back to painful experiences: the death of a loved one, betrayal by a friend, a broken relationship, the loss of a dream, and the pain and debilitation due to the sudden loss of physical health. These are moments when our faith has been stretched unbelievably thin by the realities of life.

Bitterness, anger, profound sorrow, and the darkness of those truly awful days, can re-emerge suddenly because of something we see, hear, or read.

Those moments test us...and test the progress of our healing. When faced with hardships, painful experiences, more hurt-filled losses, truly awful days, etc., can we still choose joy despite the difficulty? We often seek the face of God in the face of grief...perhaps for many days.

It is in the fires of adversity that resilience is forged. The love and strength of family and friends, hope that tomorrow can be better than yesterday, forgiveness, empathy, courage, a measure of inner strength, and our faith in the goodness and grace of God... it is all of these qualities that are melded together to develop resilience in our souls. Resilience gives us the ability to reach out to others who are hurting even as we still experience hurt. It is entirely possible to become a person who thrives despite the pain we are experiencing and have experienced.

Time absolutely does NOT heal all wounds. But over time, we figure out how to integrate our pain into our life experiences. Our pain is part of our stoxry. Debilitation is part of the human experience. But so is joy. Choose joy. Choose to thrive, not just survive.

# A Ministry of Wounded Hearts

We all have wounds. It is okay to admit that even though we live in a culture that expects us to appear invulnerable to incivility, trauma, abuse and neglect, harsh words, debilitating health problems, and other experiences that scar our souls. Occasionally, the veil to our hearts is parted and we come face to face with the depths of our own brokenness. These are powerful moments that should not be quickly dismissed even though it is disconcerting. As we grow in awareness of our own woundedness, our capacity for meaningful ministry is deepened as our empathy for others increases.

Henri Nouwen speaks an inconvenient, uncomfortable truth. We are all wounded…all of us. But this is not a weakness. On the contrary, it can be an instrument of healing for the people around us. It helps us to listen with understanding, connecting us at a heart level, and allowing us to extend care, love, and kindness in healing ways.

We live in a world full of people who are desperately seeking connection, community, acceptance, and belonging. We were already becoming a more isolated society; then the pandemic arrived, accelerating isolation to extremes.

Becoming aware of woundedness requires practiced intention and reflection. It begins with accepting our own brokenness, not shying away from it, but embracing it. We then are able to witness the healing we have experienced. It is all part of the story of God that is unfolding in us as He ministers wholeness and grace. The apostle

# The Tapestry of Life

Paul says we use the comfort we ourselves have received from God to comfort others[KS1] . This is what it means to be a wounded healer.

How can we minister the healing we have received to others today? Can we take a few moments to risk vulnerability with the intent of helping a neighbor? How can we be used as instruments of grace in the hand of God?

# **ANXIETY IS A THIEF**

I wonder how many times in our lives we allow anxiety and fear to rob us of being a blessing or being blessed. We often miss out on divine opportunities because we are shackled by our apprehensions. As we age, the accumulated life experience informs us of what MIGHT be possible, no matter how improbable a particular event might be. That is why so many people are increasingly fearful as they age. The harsh memories of past failures and disappointments cast long shadows over our courage, whispering lies about our inadequacies and limitations.

But what if we chose a different path? What if, instead of being paralyzed by fear, we chose to step out in faith? The unknown can be daunting, yet it is in these very moments of uncertainty that our faith is stretched and strengthened. Trust that God has made you more than adequate to accomplish what is hard, what may be difficult. It is in these moments where our faith grows and our confidence in God increases. Embrace the truth that God equips those He calls. His power is made perfect in our weakness, transforming our trepidation into triumph.

Time is by far our most precious commodity. Each day is made up of a succession of moments filled with potential and opportunity. How we choose to spend these moments defines the course of our lives. We can either succumb to fear or seize the day with boldness. Balance boldness with wisdom. Use this wonderful gift of time to bless others. Every second holds the possibility for us to make a difference, to touch a life, and to spread love and kindness. Do not allow uncertainty and fear dictate your decisions. Be courageous, knowing that the God of the universe is with you, that He prospers you, and favors you with His endeavors.

Imagine a life where fear no longer has a hold on you. Picture yourself embracing new relationships, stepping into new opportunities, and embarking on new ministries with a heart full of courage and a spirit anchored in faith. This is the life God calls you to live. His love casts out all fear, and His perfect peace guards your heart and mind.

So, what do you believe God is calling you to do that you are avoiding because of fear? Is it a new job, a new ministry, or perhaps reaching out to someone who needs to hear a word of encouragement? Whatever it is, know that God has already gone before you, preparing the way. Ask Him to allow you to live in His power and not to be governed by a spirit of fear. Let His strength be your foundation, His wisdom your guide, and His love your driving force.

As you reflect on this, take a moment to pray. Ask God to reveal any areas of your life where fear has taken root. Surrender these fears to Him and ask for the courage to step out in faith. Trust that He will lead you, and remember that with God, all things are possible.

May your heart be filled with boldness, your spirit with peace, and your life with the fullness of God's blessings. Step out today, not in fear, but in faith, knowing that the God who calls you is faithful. Embrace the journey, and let your life be a testament to the boundless possibilities that unfold when we trust in Him.

# Embrace Your Brokenness

People who are aware of their brokenness—who have gone through hardship and difficulty of a very personal nature, who are aware of their own fragility and mortality, who have emerged from great adversity – undergo a kind of metamorphosis. They are not the same people. They have a capacity for empathy, for connectedness, and love that is far greater than it was before their experience. They see past the facades of smiling people who are hurting, who erect barriers to keep other people out for fear of feeling the hurt. Broken people understand.

The hurt others feel runs deep. But deep calls to deep. People who are aware of their brokenness are able to love fiercely, demonstrate enormous compassion, and have developed the ability to sit, often silently, with a person in the midst of their pain and tears. The broken will run toward a person in pain, no longer uncomfortable because they have confronted the pain that belongs to them.

In some profound way, God uses broken people to be His light to others who are in the throes of truly awful experiences. They do not judge, they resist the urge to fix, and they sure do know how to attend, to bear witness to the pain, and extend great care to minister a measure of hope and wholeness.

Confronting your own brokenness is no easy thing. It is more than a tacit acknowledgment that everyone has troubles. It is learning to actively incorporate painful experiences into the narrative of one's life so that it no longer holds power over us. We become grateful for our shared lives together, understanding we have a great responsibility toward each other. Broken people value community for it is a caring community that has helped heal the wounds.

Everyone you meet is a broken person whether or not they admit it. Even the person who looks back at you in the mirror. Those who embrace their brokenness can be used in extraordinary ways in the lives of other people. Once you have walked through the dark places of your soul, you will have a new appreciation for light.

# The Treasure of People

The drive to succeed is powerful in most of us. Financial stability, a healthy retirement account, career advancement, and increasing one's personal influence, are all good things. But, oftentimes, they become ends in themselves. All of life centers around things...not people. Life is all about doing the next thing: the accomplishment of tasks for personal gain.

We have entered a time where people are often thought of as just another commodity: a means to an end. A big office, a powerful position, and personal influence are gained at the expense of people. And, in the wake of this personal success, there may be many people cast aside once their usefulness is deemed to have ended. How do these people feel? How have their lives been negatively affected? Have they been thanked for their contributions?

We need more people who spend their lives investing in people. People-helping jobs, most times, do not pay as near as well as jobs in the commercial sector. Civic group memberships are down. Mental health agencies, social work organizations, home health services, schools, and other helping entities are badly understaffed, overworked, and underpaid. The people who work in these fields are, most of the time, driven to extend compassion, care, healing, and empowerment to the increasing number of disenfranchised, "throw away" children and to adults whose lives are difficult at best.

Many people barely endure each day of life and are just trying to survive. Poverty of the wallet, but even more so, poverty of the soul, is crushing. When a person has no hope because they are continually beaten down by external realities beyond their control, they can give up and become withered and empty.

The world badly needs caring, loving people. These people see beyond the external and perceive each individual as a person of incalculable worth, deserving to be treated with dignity and respect. Sometimes it is just investing in one person. But that is how we change the world...we do it one person at a time. We bless the person, offering the "oil of gladness instead of mourning." The crown of their dignity is restored. We offer the opportunity of healing through persistent love. Listening to their stories, testifying to their hurt and pain, and offering the grace of friendship are all powerful means to reclaiming their lives and giving them hope.

Are there people within your sphere of influence that you know are hurting? How can you extend grace, compassion, and care to them today? See the person beyond their circumstances. Be a world-changer...one person at a time. You might not change the whole world, but you sure can help change their world.

# The Gift of Humility

Being humble is a difficult discipline. We are geared to put ourselves first, tending to our own happiness and advancement in life before we consider others. Our time, energy, money, thoughts, and effort are all focused on self.

Being humble, possessing a measure of humility and selflessness, is a conscious decision that must be cultivated over time. It requires a radical reorientation of how we see ourselves in the context of other selves. This recalibration means we approach life from a completely different perspective.

The guiding question in each day of our life becomes "How can I serve others today?" Humble people take great pleasure in watching other people grow. Humble people are grateful people. They do not have a need to be right. They promote the well-being of others; sometimes over their own wants and needs.

Humble people often have lived through a great trial of prolonged adversity. These experiences burn away the chaff of self-importance and bring us face to face with our own weakness and brokenness. It recalibrates how we craft our mission for each day of our life. Self is no longer the primary beneficiary of the expenditure of our resources. We seek to make a difference in the lives of people around us.

Praying for humility, for God to make us humble people, goes against human nature. But it is a way that we can follow the example of our Lord who humbled Himself during His earthly ministry.

THE TAPESTRY OF LIFE

Cultivate a humble heart. Grow in the desire to serve others without the expectation of something back from them. Love others freely and accept them as they are. Be lavish in pouring out grace to the people you see each day. Ask God to make you a blessing to someone today.

# Ministering to Suffering Souls

Why do people suffer? Why must people endure tragedy, physical and emotional pain, betrayal, debilitation, and profound grief and loss?

Throughout scripture, people suffer. Elijah was defeated and depressed. David lived in caves. Paul lived through tremendous physical hardship. Job lost everything…his wealth, family, social standing, and his health. He suffered wretchedly. We can't begin to imagine the pain and suffering of Jesus.

Why do people suffer? There are many answers. But none of them seem to matter when you are the person suffering. Suffering hurts. We can feel isolated, abandoned, and alone in our suffering.

Suffering is an intensely personal experience. The gauge of how badly people are suffering is usually based on our own periods of suffering. The responses to suffering are as varied as there are people. We often do not know how to be with people who are suffering. We are powerless to alleviate most suffering. We cannot fix it. We cannot remove it.

It is difficult to be with people who are suffering because we come face to face with our own powerlessness. We wonder how we will respond when our time to suffer arrives. Because of our own discomfort, we tell the person we will pray for them and quickly move on. How many times have you uttered such an empty promise? How can we adjust our responses to suffering so that we can be a grace to those that suffer?

People who suffer need others who will offer real help, who will stand with them in the midst of their suffering. We minister empathy, compassion, and real care that requires the expenditure of effort, and crying with them. A long hug, and a hand that holds them for a long time, a shoulder to lean on, or the ministry of presence so that the person is not left alone…these are the small graces that can make an enormous difference.

When you encounter a person who is suffering, suspend judgment on why the person is suffering. Sometimes the causes of suffering can be addressed, but more times than not, there is no fix. Do not spend your energy trying to diagnose it. Be present. Offer love and care. Genuinely pray with them…especially in their presence. Listen. Let the person know you will not abandon them in their hurt. Celebrate improvement if and when it happens. Rejoice with them when their prayers are answered. Be a small part of their journey of healing and restoration.

Suffering is a transformative experience. Elisabeth Kubler-Ross, a psychiatrist, believed that the growth that comes with recovering from suffering makes people compassionate and loving. In fact, she claimed that "the most beautiful people we have known are those who have known defeat, known suffering, known struggle, known loss, and have found their way out of the depths."[KS2] (Kübler-Ross, Elisabeth. *Death: The Final Stage of Growth*. Englewood Cliffs, NJ: Prentice-Hall, 1975)

# LOVE IS SERVING ONE ANOTHER

One enduring definition of loving others is, "can't wait to give, to serve." [KS3] Many times, the opportunity to serve comes at inconvenient moments—when we are in a hurry, when we have so much we already need to do, or when we are pressed for time. We can come up with a number of reasons just to move on—many of them reasonable, holding some degree of validity. But often these opportunities to serve are fleeting and quickly evaporate when the moment passes.

What keeps us from serving one another? Often, it is the tyranny of the urgent that pulls us away from accomplishing what is truly important. Tending to tasks becomes more important than tending to people. The to-do list screams for attention, deadlines loom, and the daily grind demands our focus. In the whirlwind of activity, the quiet call to serve others can be drowned out. Can serving be tiresome? Yes. Can we end up doing far more than we intended? Absolutely. Yet, in those moments of selfless service, we often find a deeper fulfillment and purpose.

But as we approach life from an eternal perspective, God has a passion for people, period. Not for paperwork or policies or programs. Not for the accomplishment of tasks that are divorced from the well-being of others. People. When we read the Gospels, we see Jesus constantly putting people first. He took time for the marginalized, the sick, and the outcast. He saw them, acknowledged them,

# The Tapestry of Life

and served them. His life was a testament to the profound truth that the purpose of human life is to serve.

Albert Schweitzer's quote is spot on: "The purpose of human life is to serve, and to show compassion and the will to help others." (Schweitzer, Albert. *The Philosophy of Civilization*. Translated by C. T. Campion. New York: Macmillan, 1949) [KS4] His last phrase is key— "the will to help others"—implies a choice, an intentional orientation away from ourselves, our own needs, our own benefit, and turning our focus and energies to the well-being of other people. It is truly a place where the smallest of deeds is better than the greatest of intentions. A kind word, a listening ear, or a helping hand—these seemingly insignificant actions can make a world of difference.

We will all have many opportunities to serve today. These opportunities may not come with fanfare or recognition. They may not fit conveniently into our schedules or align with our plans. They may take the sacrificial giving of our time and energy in a way in which we will derive no benefit for ourselves. But we may change the world for the better for one person. And in doing so, we align ourselves with God's heart for humanity.

How can we serve others today? How can we extend grace and compassion in real, tangible ways? It might be as simple as offering a smile to a stranger, helping a neighbor with groceries, or taking a moment to truly listen to someone who is hurting. These acts of service, though small, have the power to ripple out and create a wave of kindness and love in our communities.

In serving others, we are not only fulfilling a divine mandate but also enriching our own lives. Service is a profound act of worship, a way to live out our faith in the most practical terms. It is an expression of love that speaks louder than words and touches hearts in ways that we may never fully understand.

So, let us embrace the opportunities to serve, even when they come at inconvenient times. Let us choose to be people who can't wait to give, to serve. In doing so, we make our little corners of the world a better place, one act of kindness at a time. And perhaps, in serving others, we will find ourselves growing closer to the heart of God, experiencing the joy and fulfillment that comes from living a life of compassion and love.

# The Precious Gift of Life

Life is an unspeakably precious gift we have the privilege of enjoying each day. Every day. With the rising of the sun, we rise... to experience a brand-new gift of twenty-four unblemished hours, full of possibilities and potential.

Many of us have had a brush with our own mortality. Whether it be a very serious health problem, a near-miss traffic accident, or a work-related accident...some of us have come right up to the very precipice of our existence and have been able to walk back from death's grasp. Often times, those experiences result in physical limitations or emotional scars that will be with us for the rest of our lives here on planet Earth. But they are reminders of what could have happened, mentors that teach us to treasure every moment, every breath.

Those experiences drive home how good, and how precious life is. Such experiences bring forth great gratitude for the joy of one more day with our spouses, one more day with our families, one more day of companionship with our friends and co-workers, one more day to make a difference, one more day to relish life on God's good Earth, one more day to forgive and be forgiven, and one more day to experience and extend grace.

Even our hardships remind us we are alive; we are still here. We do not need to wait for the hardships to end in order to be joy-filled. Difficulty brings clarity and helps us appreciate our lives in ways we did not prior to adversity. We may even grow to the point where we become grateful for suffering, for it helps to be grateful that we are alive for one more day.

This is a game-changing paradigm shift in how we approach our days. But watch what happens to you, and to those around you, as you walk in gratitude. It is, perhaps, the key characteristic whereby a genuine child of God is recognized.

When was the last time you expressed unbridled, unconditional gratitude to God for life? For the joy of just being alive? For the tremendous blessings we enjoy each day? Live in gratitude today. Choose joy. Be kind and compassionate. Make no demands of God or others. Just enjoy being. Thank God throughout your day for life.

# You Matter!

Our society has done us all a great disservice by diminishing the worth of individual people. If you are not part of the right voting bloc, part of the proper demographic, or have not amassed a great personal fortune, you, as a person, will have been told you don't matter. Even in churches, especially in churches, people's individual worth to a congregation is measured by their contributions of time, energy, and especially, money. When was the last time you saw a person recognized solely for their faithful attendance in church?

Schools recognize only the A students or stellar athletes who go on to play collegiate ball. Companies and organizations center on a handful of the most gifted, most productive employees. Poorer communities do not have as varied of selections of healthy foods at their nationwide grocery chains because less nutritious food is cheaper… leading to health problems among a marginalized community. Whole clothing chains sell apparel that will fit only a small portion of the public who have whatever body type is currently in vogue.

Our society is brutal in the way people are marginalized and thrown away. Look what is happening to our children! Horrible, awful things are said to them over social media. And they believe it. As a result, depression and suicide rates are rising among tweens and teens.

And people with intellectual and developmental disabilities are barely recognized as people. They receive inferior medical treatment, live in homes most of us would not even enter, and are treated as if they were discardable human beings.

Psalm 139 sets the record straight. EVERY person matters. EVERY person is created uniquely, and individually by God Himself. EVERY person bears His image. EVERY person is a fresh thought from God. God made you with a gift set that is entirely your own. You reflect the glory of God in a singular way. Each person is made to transcribe the glory of God into creation in a unique fashion. When you die, something very precious is taken from creation and existence is diminished by your loss.

You matter! YOU MATTER! Some people are not more valuable than other people. All people are of incalculable worth. There is no such thing as an inconsequential ministry. All ministries matter. As the song says, "If it matters to you, it matters to the Master."[KS5]

How can we affirm the worth of people around us today, regardless of who they are or what they do? What can we say or do that will raise up those that have been beaten up by a cruel, uncaring world?

Be a refuge, a haven. Provide safe harbor to those around you today. Care for their personhood. Listen. Tend to their souls. Let everyone we meet today know that they are loved by God and by us.

# Walking in Gratitude

Gratitude is always the response to grace. The more we reflect on how blessed we are, the greater our capacity is to walk in gratitude. Every day, we experience an abundance of graces.

If you rise from your bed in the morning, can walk without assistance, have people in your life who you love and who love you, a job where you earn money and enjoy your fellow co-workers, a roof over your head, a car that you drive, and the ability to draw each breath along with every beat of your heart... if you have experienced any of these, even one time...you are blessed. You have experienced grace. Abundant graces. And grace is ALWAYS amazing.

Consider your blessings. Expand your ability to receive grace, even if it isn't the grace you think you want or need. Grace is grace. Grace is always good. This will cause you to become increasingly grateful. It will transform you with your soul ever increasingly becoming more and more richly textured. Gratitude, over time, will blossom from your heart. It will not be fake or forced, but rather, it will flow from a genuine understanding of the grace in which we are immersed.

Gratitude recalibrates the entire orientation of our lives. It is a faithful companion in all the seasons of our lives. A grateful person blesses the people they encounter.

Take a few moments to reflect on the many graces you receive each day. What are the blessings you experience? How could you express gratitude for the grace you receive? What does "walking in gratitude" look like for you?

Give thanks with a grateful heart...

# Embracing the Outsider: Love Over Judgment

In a world marked by division and difference, we often find ourselves grappling with the concept of "other-ness." Whether it's the way someone dresses, the beliefs they hold, or the life choices they make, it's easy to fall into the trap of judgment. Yet, as followers of Christ, we are called to a higher standard: to offer love and acceptance; to bless the personhood of every individual with dignity and respect.

Consider the life of Jesus. He consistently chose love over judgment. When He encountered the Samaritan woman at the well, He did not condemn her for her past or her choices. Instead, He engaged with her, offering her living water and treating her with profound respect (John 4:1-26). Jesus saw beyond her "other-ness" and recognized her inherent worth as a child of God.

In our daily lives, we encounter people who seem different from us. It's easy to let preconceived notions cloud our interactions; to let judgment creep into our hearts. But what if we chose to see every person as Jesus sees them? What if we recognized their struggles, their humanity, and their intrinsic value?

Imagine the transformative power of looking at someone and, instead of critiquing their differences, embracing their uniqueness. When we offer love and acceptance, we reflect the heart of God. We create a space where people feel seen and valued, where their dignity is upheld, and their personhood is affirmed.

This isn't always easy. Our instincts might push us towards judgment, especially when someone's choices or lifestyle starkly contrast with our own values. Yet, it's precisely in these moments that the call to love becomes most critical. To bless someone's personhood means to see them as God sees them—fearfully and wonderfully made (Psalm 139:14), and worthy of love and grace.

The act of offering acceptance and respect does not mean we endorse every behavior or belief. Rather, it means we choose to see the person first. We acknowledge their journey, their struggles, and their story. We extend the same grace that we ourselves have received.

When we encounter "other-ness", it becomes an opportunity to demonstrate Christ's love. Think of the tax collector Zacchaeus. He was despised and judged by many, yet Jesus invited him to share a meal, treating him with honor and kindness (Luke 19:1-10). That act of acceptance transformed Zacchaeus' life.

Similarly, our acts of love and respect can have a profound impact. When we offer a listening ear, a kind word, or a simple gesture of respect, we plant seeds of grace. We break down walls of division and build bridges of understanding. In doing so, we reflect the kingdom of God, where every person is valued and loved.

So, let us strive to offer love instead of judgment. Let us bless each person with the dignity and respect they deserve. By doing so, we mirror the boundless love of our Creator, drawing others closer to His heart. May our lives be a testament to the power of acceptance; a beacon of Christ's love in a world that desperately needs it.

# Become Who You Are

It is very difficult to differentiate who you really are from who you are supposed to be. Many of us struggle in life to be the person we are told we need to be, rather than be who we really are. Several people—when they reach their thirties, forties, or even fifties—find that, though they are making a great deal of money and have successful careers, they are unhappy, hollow, bereft of purpose, and are unfulfilled. Why is that?

It's because they have lived their lives according to what a person, or group of people, told them they should be. They have made all the "proper" expected life progressions: high school, college, job, career, marriage… These expectations are imposed on us from a very young age. Instead of becoming who God created us to be, we follow a path set before us by someone else. We live out someone else's idea for our lives. Many people die having lived out a life not their own.

How can we become who we are rather than who we are supposed to be? How can we move from a place of being unfulfilled to one of joy-filled purpose that results from being who we are?

Discover your call. Discover YOUR call. People who are truly happy with their lives, who have a deep sense of meaning and purpose, who live their lives to fulfill their mission…these people live within their call.

Part of the joy of growing up is discovering one's call. How one goes about that is different for each person, because each person's call is unique. God has made you for a purpose and placed a call on your life.

You are here for a reason because God wants to accomplish something through you that no other person can. You are here at this time in this place because, from before the creation of the world, God had already decided when and where to bring you into being.

You are here for a reason…perhaps many reasons.

Calls are generally multifaceted and there is certainly more than one way to live out one's call.

People who live their calls are deeply content people. Their lives always "point north", so to speak. They have direction, bearing, and a confidence not born of self, but given to them by God.

A prime example of all of this can be found in the fields of education and social work. A person may be thriving as a teacher in the classroom. They may be outstanding clinicians. They are helping many, many people. Then, they are appointed a vice-principal or given an administrative posting. And these brilliant, gifted people flop big time in their new roles. They become unhappy, miserable people. They have made an expected career progression, but it caused them to leave their call. They return back to their place of evident blessing and go on to continue living happy lives with a little bit more of life wisdom.

These uncomfortable moments are used by God to affirm His call in our lives.

Have confidence in God, the Author of your life and the Bishop of your soul. If you are unhappy because you are trying to be who you are supposed to be instead of the person God created you to be, ask the Lord to bring your life into alignment with His call.

This may not be easy. It is certainly not a linear process. And it may take years. But God always gets us to where He wants us to go. Have an unfailing confidence that God accompanies you through all the days of your life. Ask Him for the grace to live in His call.

Become who YOU are.

# The Difference Between Guilt and Shame

What is the difference between guilt and shame?

In *Shame Interrupted*, Ed Welch writes, "Guilt's message is, 'I did something bad,' and needs justification and forgiveness."[KS6] (Welch, Edward T. *Shame Interrupted: How God Lifts the Pain of Worthlessness and Rejection.* Greensboro, NC: New Growth Press, 2012.) Shame's message is, 'I am bad,' and it needs an identity shift and relational connection. Shame feels like it's welded onto you. Shame is what lingers even after we have asked God for forgiveness. It is a product of our own actions which we must face.

But a more insidious source of shame arises when your personhood has been sinned against by someone else. You may have been demeaned, belittled, ridiculed, or shunned. Many people have suffered abuse during the course of their lives. Those wounds run deep, are slow to heal, and cause profound sorrow and shame.

So many people are staggering under the crushing weight of shame. They have no idea how to get out from under it. They are mortified at the thought of sharing the burden with someone else. They do not know where to go for help. And so, this drives them deeper into fear, loneliness, and isolation.

Oftentimes, a person will try to bury something that gave rise to shame in their childhood and will still be carrying it with them twenty, thirty, or forty years later. It is a source of constant grief and affects all of life, robbing them of many opportunities to experience joy and inhibiting the formation of healthy, meaningful relationships.

Heather Nelson, in her book *Unashamed,* writes, "Shame disappears in community. The most powerful way to combat shame is to be truly known and to know others truly. As we share our shame stories or the ways that shame has threatened to silence us—and these stories are met with compassionate empathy—shame fades away. It loses the fuel of isolation and fear."[KS7] (Nelson, Heather Davis. *Unashamed: Healing Our Brokenness and Finding Freedom from Shame.* Wheaton, IL: Crossway, 2016.)

Acceptance and belonging, forgiveness, accountability, and the opportunity to live differently tomorrow than they did yesterday are key elements that need to exist in a community for a person to heal and grow. These elements are part of a healthy Christian community.

Sharing our own brokenness, confessing our own sin, and allowing the person to enter into our own journey of forgiveness and acceptance, shines the light of hope in the darkness created by shame.

You can be a broken healer. You can be a difference-maker in someone's life. You can be an instrument of healing grace as you listen to their story, offer acceptance and belonging, and accompany them to a place of healing and rest for their soul.

# Hearing the Voice of God

For over one hundred years, a man was ridiculed and criticized by the people around him. Day after day, he endured the jeers and the sneers, the harsh words and the skeptical looks. He was the subject of mockery and disbelief. But for one hundred years, he also heard his Creator tell him to continue in the work He had given him. Amid the cacophony of doubt and derision, a still, small voice spoke words of encouragement and purpose. This man chose to listen and obey his Creator, not his critics. And, in the end, he helped save humanity.

This man was Noah.

Imagine the world Noah lived in—a world filled with corruption, violence, and disregard for the divine. Yet, over the din of the world, Noah heard the voice of his Creator. It wasn't a thunderous command but a gentle, persistent whisper that penetrated his heart. He obeyed humbly and without question. With each hammer blow and plank he laid; Noah stood firm in his faith. He did so through a relentless storm of criticism, the laughter of his neighbors echoing in his ears, and the disbelief of those closest to him weighing on his heart.

And God was faithful to him. Through Noah's obedience, the course of history was altered. God blessed the world through him, sparing a remnant of life from the deluge that was to come. The ark became a symbol of God's grace and salvation; a testament to what happens when one person dares to trust and obey the Creator, even when it seems like madness to everyone else.

Trust your Creator with each moment, even in difficulty. When the storms of life rage around you, when the voices of doubt and criticism grow loud, remember that God's love for us continues unabated. He sees the end from the beginning, and His plans for us are woven with threads of purpose and love. Pay attention to your Creator. In the midst of chaos, let His voice be the one that guides you. Know that you are created with purpose, a unique calling that only you can fulfill. Live in the call God has placed on your life.

Obeying God is more than an act of duty; it is a profound way of worshiping Him with your life. It is saying, "I trust You more than I trust the opinions of others. I believe in Your promises more than the evidence of my circumstances." And it is a way God uses you to bless the people around you. Your obedience can be the vessel through which God's grace flows to others.

Do you hear the voice of God? He speaks through His creation: the gentle rustle of leaves, the majesty of mountains, and the serenity of a sunrise. We have His very words in our Bibles; a love letter written across time and space. And the Creator God of Genesis, the One Who upholds all things by the power of His word, chooses to live in His children. This God, who spun galaxies into existence, is intimately involved in our lives. He is speaking clearly, continuously because He loves us and desires a relationship with us.

Over the din of your world, through the storms of criticism you face, may you hear and heed the voice of God today. Let His words be your anchor, His promises your refuge. Just as Noah found strength and purpose in the midst of his trials, may you find courage and direction in the gentle, unwavering voice of your Creator.

# Compassion Fatigue

We live in a broken world full of broken people. We all have responses when we experience brokenness. Some will try to ignore it, some will try to escape, and some will use humor or other means to divert their attention away from it, but many of us will try to fix what is broken. People will flock to fixers because they are good at fixing many situations.

A problem at work, a soured relationship, a difficult boss, a button that needs sewing back on, or finding a misplaced cellphone...a myriad of needs, both great and small, are faced by fixers. They will refrain from tending to their own needs as they pour themselves into addressing the needs of others. And it doesn't stop. The needs of others inundate this good soul day after day because a fixer is lousy at saying the word "No"...and meaning it.

The desire to help others is a noble calling. But people who fix...which is different than serving...quickly burn out. They shut down out of self-preservation and then need "fixing" themselves. So, what is a fixer to do besides not fixing everything?

People who help others...who serve others...need times of rest to replenish themselves. This rest is not just physical, but emotional and spiritual as well. It requires you to find a place, both physically and mentally, where you are away from the crush of the world, and you can just be.

Access to places of great grandeur...mountains or oceans...are often places where our souls can rest. But vacations happen only a couple of times a year. The trick is to find or even create places and spaces that can be frequently accessed where you can soulfully rest. It is here where you experience a measure of peace.

Exercise venues, your backyard perhaps with a fire pit in the evening, the night sky, a local lake or river, the library or bookstore, a special place where you pray, your church and church family, a drive in the country, or sitting outside on your porch, cooking, gardening, fishing...there are many places of physical and soulful rest available. You must choose to discover and use them.

God created us to work and to serve one another. But He also created us to rest, replenish, and enjoy Him. And so, we find time, places, and spaces for both. "Blessed are the balanced." May you be blessed as God graces you with balance and peace.

# THE COURAGE OF VULNERABILITY

In the quiet corners of our hearts, where silent suffering often takes refuge, there lies a hidden strength waiting to be discovered: the courage of vulnerability. It is a delicate, powerful act to reveal our deepest fears, doubts, and wounds to others. In a world that celebrates strength and independence, admitting our need for help can feel like a daunting, even impossible, task.

Imagine standing on the edge of a vast ocean; the waves crashing against the shore, relentless and unyielding. This is how our struggles can feel—overwhelming and insurmountable. Yet, in the face of such formidable forces, there is a profound beauty in allowing ourselves to be vulnerable. It's like stepping into those waves, not with the intent to conquer them alone, but to embrace their power and trust that we will not be swept away.

Vulnerability is an act of immense bravery. It's a declaration that we are human, that we hurt, and that we cannot walk this path alone. In 2 Corinthians 12:9, Paul hears the Lord's gentle reminder: "My grace is sufficient for you, for my power is made perfect in weakness." This truth illuminates our hearts: in our moments of greatest weakness, God's strength shines the brightest. When we dare to be vulnerable, we open the door for divine power to work within us.

Reflect on the night in the Garden of Gethsemane, where Jesus, knowing the agony that lay ahead, chose to lay bare His soul before His disciples. "My soul is overwhelmed with sorrow to the point of death," He confessed (Matthew 26:38). This moment of raw vulnerability, from the Son of God Himself, teaches us that there is no shame in expressing our deepest sorrows and fears. Instead, it is an act of courage that draws us closer to the heart of God and those around us.

The courage of vulnerability creates bonds of empathy and connection. When we open up about our struggles, we often discover that others are walking similar paths. Our honesty becomes a radiant source of hope, inviting others to step into the light and share their own burdens. Galatians 6:2 calls us to "carry each other's burdens, and in this way, you will fulfill the law of Christ." This mutual sharing is where true community is born; a place where love and support flourish.

Vulnerability also paves the way for healing. In James 5:16, we are encouraged to "confess your sins to each other and pray for each other so that you may be healed." This principle extends beyond sin to all areas of our lives where we need God's grace and the support of our community. When we bring our hidden wounds into the open, we allow the healing light of Christ to touch them, fostering restoration and wholeness.

If you are carrying silent suffering, let the courage of vulnerability guide you. Share your struggles with God in prayer and reach out to trusted friends or family. In this brave act, you will discover a strength that transcends your fears, a community that uplifts you, and a God who meets you in your weakness with His perfect power. Through the courage of vulnerability, we transform our silent suffering into a journey of profound growth and healing.

# Silent Suffering

There is a kind of suffering that remains hidden, buried beneath the surface of daily life, and masked by the façade of normalcy. It's the kind that doesn't scream for attention but whispers quietly, incessantly. Silent suffering is the pain that gnaws at the soul when no one is watching, the crying that dampens the pillow in the privacy of night, and the ache that lingers in the heart long after the world has moved on. It's the agony that we carry alone, feeling unseen and unheard.

Silent suffering is a burden many carry, often unnoticed by those around them. It's the grief that lacks words, the despair that hides behind smiles, and the tears that never fall in public. In a world where we are encouraged to share our struggles openly, there remains a significant number of us who endure our pain quietly, feeling as if our silent suffering is unseen and unheard.

The Bible contains the accounts of many people who suffered in silence. Consider the story of Hannah. She longed for a child, and her suffering was deep and personal. When she went to the temple to pray, her lips moved, but her voice was silent. Eli, the priest, saw her and thought she was drunk because her prayers were so silent and fervent. But God saw her heart and heard her silent cries (1 Sam. 1:10–17). God answered her prayers, showing that even our quietest cries reach His ears.

Silent suffering can feel isolated. We may believe that no one understands our pain or that our struggles are too insignificant to share. However, Psalm 56:8 reminds us that God collects every tear in His bottle and records them in His book. This imagery assures us that our silent suffering is precious to God. He sees every tear, hears every unspoken word, and understands every bit of pain.

When words fail, and we have nothing left but our raw, unfiltered pain, we are invited to lean into His presence. In our silent suffering, we can find a deep sense of intimacy with God. It is in these quiet interludes that we can pour out our hearts to Him without fear of judgment or misunderstanding. God invites us to come to Him with all our burdens. Matthew 11:28–29 says, "Come to me, all you who are weary and burdened, and I will give you rest. Take my yoke upon you and learn from me, for I am gentle and humble in heart, and you will find rest for your souls." In our silence, we find His gentle invitation to rest, to be held, and to be healed.

Silent suffering forces us into a place of profound dependence on God. When we have no words left, we are forced to rely entirely on God. It strips away the superficial, leaving us with nothing but our need for Him. In this sacred space, we discover a God who is not distant but near; a God who is not indifferent but deeply compassionate. "The Lord is close to the brokenhearted and saves those who are crushed in spirit" (Ps. 34:18). It is in our most silent, solitary moments of suffering that we often feel His presence most acutely.

We can also find comfort in the knowledge that Jesus Himself experienced silent suffering. In the Garden of Gethsemane, He prayed in agony, His sweat like drops of blood falling to the ground (Luke 22:44). On the cross, He endured the ultimate silent suffering, feeling abandoned even by God. Yet, through His suffering, He brought redemption to the world. Our silent suffering, too, can become a channel of God's grace and strength, bearing witness to His enduring love.

As we navigate our silent suffering, let us remember that we are not alone. God is with us, listening to our silent prayers and holding us close. Our silent suffering can become a powerful testimony of

God's faithfulness and love. Let us find strength in His presence and trust that He is working in ways we cannot see.

In our silent suffering, we find the quiet assurance that we are deeply known, deeply loved, and never, ever alone. Our silent suffering grows into a sacred communion with the God who sees, who hears, and who heals.

# Resting in God

In our fast-paced world, the idea of rest can sometimes feel like a luxury we can't afford. We're constantly on the go, juggling multiple responsibilities, and trying to keep up with the demands of everyday life. But, in the midst of this busyness, God offers us a different kind of rest—a rest that goes beyond physical relaxation to bring deep satisfaction to our souls.

When we talk about resting in God, we're not just talking about taking a break from our work or finding a quiet moment in our day. We're talking about entering into a state of being where we trust God completely, where we surrender our worries and fears to Him, and where we find our true identity and purpose in Him.

Resting in God is more than a pause in our day; it's an immersion into the depths of His love and grace. It's a journey into the heart of our Creator, where the noise of the world fades away, and all that remains is the sweet embrace of His presence.

This kind of rest brings a deep satisfaction that can't be found anywhere else. It's a satisfaction that comes from knowing that we are loved unconditionally by our Creator, that we are valued and cherished just as we are. It's a satisfaction that comes from being in His presence, from experiencing His peace and His joy in the midst of life's ups and downs.

Imagine yourself standing on the shore of a vast ocean; the waves gently lapping at your feet. As you close your eyes and breathe in the salty air, you feel a sense of peace wash over you. This is the kind of peace that comes from resting in God—a peace that surpasses all understanding, a peace that fills your soul to the brim and overflows into every corner of your being.

When we rest in God, we find that our souls are nourished and refreshed. We find that we can face life's challenges with a sense of peace and confidence, knowing that God is with us and that He is working all things together for our good (Rom. 8:28). We find that we no longer need to strive to earn God's love or to prove our worth, because we know that we are already loved and accepted by Him.

In this place of rest, you are free to be yourself, without fear or pretense. You can lay down your burdens, your worries, your doubts, and allow God to take them from you. You can open your heart fully to Him, knowing that you are safe in His hands, knowing that He cares for you deeply and tenderly.

As you rest in God, you begin to see yourself and the world around you through His eyes. You see the beauty of His creation, the wonder of His love, and the majesty of His grace. You are filled with awe and gratitude, and your heart overflows with praise.

The journey of resting in God is not always easy. There are times when the storms of life rage around us, when the waves threaten to overwhelm us. But even in the midst of the storm, God is there, offering us His hand, and inviting us to rest in Him.

This deep satisfaction is not dependent on our circumstances. It doesn't come from having everything in our lives perfectly in order or from achieving all of our goals. Rather, it comes from knowing that we are secure in God's love, that His plans for us are good, and that He is always with us, guiding us, and sustaining us through every moment of our lives.

So, as you go about your day, take some time to rest in God. Allow yourself to be still in His presence, to soak in His love and His peace. Allow yourself to experience the deep satisfaction that comes from resting in Him and let that satisfaction overflow into every area of your life.

# WHO DEFINES YOU?

In a world that constantly bombards us with messages about who we should be, it's easy to fall into the trap of letting external factors define our identity. We're told that our worth is tied to our achievements, our relationships, our appearance, our education, or our social status. But is that truly where our identity lies?

The truth is, our identity is not defined by these external factors, but by something much deeper and more enduring. As Christians, we believe that our true identity is found in our relationship with God. In the book of Genesis, we are told that we are created in the image of God. This means that our worth and value come from being loved and cherished by our Creator, not from anything we do or achieve.

In the New Testament, the apostle Paul writes to the church in Ephesus, reminding them of their true identity in Christ. He tells them that they are "God's handiwork, created in Christ Jesus to do good works, which God prepared in advance for us to do" (Ephesians 2:10, NIV). This passage reminds us that our identity is not based on what we have done or what others think of us, but on the fact that we are beloved children of God, created for a purpose.

When we allow external factors to define us, we can easily fall into the trap of comparison and competition. We may feel that we are never good enough, that we always have to do more, or be more, to be accepted. But when we understand that our identity comes from God, we can find freedom from this endless striving. We can rest in the knowledge that we are already accepted and loved just as we are.

This doesn't mean that we should ignore our talents and abilities, or that we shouldn't strive to be the best version of ourselves. But it does mean that we should not let these things become the sole source of our identity. Our worth is not dependent on what we do, but on who we are in Christ.

So, the next time you find yourself feeling defined by your achievements, your relationships, or your circumstances, remember that your true identity is found in God. You are loved, you are valued, and you are enough, just as you are.

# Grappling with Doubt

In the journey of faith, doubt can be a companion as familiar as the air we breathe. We often wrestle with questions that seem to chip away at the foundation of our beliefs, leaving us feeling vulnerable and unsure. But what if, instead of seeing doubt as a weakness, we view it as a natural part of our faith journey, a pathway to deeper understanding and a stronger foundation?

Doubt is not a sign of weakness, but of our humanity. It's the trembling of our hearts as we confront the grand mysteries of God, the questions that have no easy answers. It's the ache in our spirits as we grapple with suffering and injustice, wondering where God is in the midst of it all. It's the silent scream of our souls as we confront the silence of God, longing for a word, a sign, anything to assure us that we are not alone.

Doubt, in its essence, is a recognition of the limits of our understanding. It's a humbling acknowledgment that we do not have all the answers. This recognition can lead us to a place of openness, where we are more receptive to the mysteries of faith. It can invite us to explore our beliefs more deeply, to seek out the truths that resonate most deeply with our souls.

Our faith, like fragile glass, may appear delicate and easily shattered by the storms of doubt. Yet, it is in these moments of doubt that our faith can grow stronger, much like tempered glass that becomes tougher through the process of heating and cooling. Doubt can refine our beliefs, burning away the impurities and leaving behind a faith that is more resilient and genuine.

The Bible is filled with stories of doubt and faith intertwined, like two lovers locked in a dance. Abraham doubted that he would ever have a son, yet he trusted in God's promise and became the father of nations. Moses doubted his ability to lead his people out of Egypt, yet he followed God's call and became a liberator. Peter doubted his own courage, yet he became a rock upon which the church was built. Thomas, often referred to as "Doubting Thomas," doubted the resurrection of Jesus until he saw the wounds on His hands and side. His doubt was met with compassion and understanding, and he was invited to touch the wounds, leading to a deeper faith and understanding.

Our faith, like theirs, is not a static thing, but a journey, a pilgrimage of doubt and faith, of questions and answers, and of darkness and light. It's a journey that leads us deeper into the heart of God, where we discover that our doubts are not a barrier to faith, but a bridge to a deeper, more intimate relationship with our Creator.

So let us embrace our doubts, not as a sign of weakness, but as a pathway to a deeper, more authentic faith. Let us allow our doubts to lead us on a journey of discovery, where we may find that our faith is stronger and more beautiful because of its frailty. Let us not cling to what only our eyes can see but embrace the beauty of the unknown. For it's in those periods of doubt, when our faith trembles like a leaf in the wind, that we discover the true depth of our relationship with God, and His boundless love that sustains us.

# The Crucible of Suffering

In the tapestry of life, there are moments when the fabric of our existence is torn asunder, leaving us exposed to the rawness of our vulnerability. It's in these days, weeks, or years that we come face to face with the fragility of our health, the impermanence of our relationships, and the transient nature of our worldly possessions. What we once held dear—our sight, our mobility, our very breath—can be snatched away in the blink of an eye, leaving us gasping for air, both literally and figuratively.

For those who believe such tragedies could never befall them, reality can be a brutal awakening. The ground beneath our feet crumbles, and we are left suspended in a void of uncertainty, where every thought, every action, every breath is filtered through a lens of pain and discomfort. The future we once envisioned is shrouded in a haze of doubt and fear.

Suddenly, every aspect of life is tinged with suffering and loss. Tasks that once seemed mundane now require herculean effort. Simple pleasures become elusive, overshadowed by the weight of our circumstances. When faced with such daunting circumstances, courage becomes not just a virtue but a necessity. It is what propels us forward, urging us not to succumb to despair but to take one small, courageous step forward each day. It is the silent strength that sustains us when all other lights have dimmed, guiding us through the darkest of nights.

But courage alone is not enough. It is the love of family, the compassion of friends, and the unwavering grace of God that lifts us

# The Tapestry of Life

up when we have fallen, that bind our wounds when we are broken, and that remind us that we are never truly alone.

And so, we persevere. We fight against the tide of despair, clinging to the hope that lies just beyond our reach. We learn to find joy in the small victories, in the moments of respite from pain, and in the laughter that pierces the darkness like a ray of sunshine.

And when, at last, we emerge from the crucible of our suffering, we are not the same. We are stronger, more resilient, and more grateful for the blessings that surround us. We have learned to cherish the simple pleasures, to savor each moment, and to embrace life with a newfound fervor.

As we look back on our journey, we see not just the pain and the struggle, but also the moments of grace, of love, and of profound beauty that emerged from the darkness. We are reminded that life is a tapestry woven from both joy and sorrow, and that it is in facing our trials with courage and grace that we truly come to understand the depth of our own strength.

So, to all those who find themselves in the midst of hardship, I say this: hold fast to hope. Know that you are not alone, that your pain is seen and felt. Your courage and fortitude bear witness to your resilience and faith in God. May God minister healing to you… mind, body, and soul. May you experience great grace to sustain you as you traverse the wilderness of suffering. Rest in the knowledge that you are greatly loved. And may the light of God's joy, the light of His presence, shine brightly in your heart.

# Cultivating Humility

Being humble is a difficult discipline. We are geared to put ourselves first, tending to our own happiness and advancement in life before we consider others. Our time, energy, money, thoughts, and effort are all focused on self.

Being humble, possessing a measure of humility and selflessness, is a conscious decision that must be cultivated over time. It requires a radical reorientation of how we see ourselves in the context of other selves. This recalibration means we approach life from a completely different perspective.

The guiding question each day of our life becomes "How can I serve others today?" Humble people take great pleasure in watching other people grow. Humble people are grateful people. They do not have a need to be right. They promote the well-being of others, sometimes over their own wants and needs.

Humble individuals often emerge from enduring long seasons of intense struggle. These challenges strip away the excess of pride, revealing our true fragility and imperfections. This process redefines our daily intentions, shifting our focus away from self-centeredness. Instead, we become driven by a desire to positively impact and support the lives of those around us.Humble people often have lived through a great trial of prolonged adversity. These experiences burn away the chaff of self-importance and bring us face to face with our own weakness and brokenness. It recalibrates how we craft our mission for each day of our life. Self is no longer the primary beneficiary of the expenditure of our resources. We seek to make a difference in the lives of people around us.[KS8]

Praying for humility, for God to make us humble people, goes against human nature. But it is a way we can follow the example of our Lord who humbled Himself during His earthly ministry.

Cultivate a humble heart. Grow in the desire to serve others without the expectation of something back from them. Love others freely and accept them as they are. Be lavish in pouring out grace to the people you see each day. Ask God to make you a blessing to someone today.

# Embracing our Brokenness

In the journey of life, we all encounter moments that shatter us, leaving us fragmented and vulnerable. These moments, though painful, have the potential to transform us in remarkable ways. People who have embraced their brokenness, who have traversed the depths of hardship and emerged on the other side, undergo a profound metamorphosis. They are not the same; they are more.

Through their own experiences of suffering, broken individuals develop a heightened sense of empathy and understanding. They see beyond the masks that others wear, reaching out to those who are hurting with a depth of compassion that can only come from having felt that same pain themselves. Their hearts are open, their ears attentive, and their presence is a source of comfort to those in need.

God often uses these broken vessels as His instruments of light and hope in the lives of others. They do not offer judgment or quick fixes but instead provide a safe space for others to express their pain and find solace. In their brokenness, they become beacons of love, demonstrating the beauty of compassion and the power of simply being there for someone in their darkest hour.

As Christians, we believe that Jesus himself was broken for us; his body broken on the cross so that we might be made whole. It is through his brokenness that we find healing, redemption, and restoration. As we walk in his footsteps, we are called to embrace our own brokenness, knowing that it is through our brokenness that God's light shines most brightly.

Confronting our own brokenness is a daunting task. It requires us to not only acknowledge our pain but also to integrate it into the fabric of our lives, transforming it from a source of suffering into a wellspring of empathy and wisdom. It is a journey of healing, one that is often guided by the supportive hands of a caring community.

Indeed, community plays a vital role in the lives of the broken. It is within the embrace of a loving community that healing begins, where wounds are tended to, and hope is restored. Through shared experiences and mutual support, broken individuals find strength and resilience, enabling them to not only survive their hardships, but also to thrive in spite of them.

As we navigate the complexities of life, let us remember that everyone we meet is carrying a burden, whether visible or hidden. By embracing our own brokenness and extending compassion to others, we can become agents of healing and transformation in a world that is desperately in need of light. Through our brokenness, we can shine brightly, illuminating the path for others as they journey through their own dark nights of the soul.

Once you have walked through the dark places of your soul, you will have a new appreciation for light.

# Becoming Stuck in Grief

In the tapestry of life, grief is a thread we all must weave. It's a natural response to loss, a testament to the depth of our love and the richness of our relationships. In the quiet corners of our hearts, grief often takes root, planting itself as a natural response to loss. Yet, there are times when grief's sorrowful tendrils extend deeper, wrapping around our very being, morphing into something heavier—depression.

Grief is a journey, a path we reluctantly tread, lined with memories of what once was. It's a process of coming to terms with the absence of what we cherished, a struggle to find meaning in the midst of loss. Initially, grief can feel like a storm, fierce and overwhelming, but as time passes, its intensity softens, allowing for moments of light to filter through the clouds.

However, for some, this storm never seems to abate. The heavy cloak of sadness becomes a constant companion, weighing down every thought and action. What was once a natural part of the grieving process transforms into something deeper, darker, and more sinister—depression.

Depression is a thief of joy, a relentless shadow that distorts our perception of reality. It robs us of hope, leaving us adrift in a sea of despair. The things that once brought us comfort now seem distant and unattainable. We feel lost, disconnected from the world around us, as if we're watching life pass by from behind a thick veil.

As Christians, we are not immune to the pain of grief. We, too, experience the ache of loss, the emptiness of absence. We know what it is to mourn, to long for the touch of a loved one who is no longer with us. Some of our brothers and sisters become stuck in their grief. It is there where the grief stagnates, sours, and turns into the greater darkness of depression.

In the midst of our darkest moments, it can be hard to see a way out. Depression clouds our vision, distorting our perception of reality. It can feel as if we are trapped in a never-ending cycle of sadness and despair.

The journey from grief to healing is not a linear path; it's a winding road with twists and turns, ups and downs. It's a journey that requires patience, courage, and a deep trust in God's plan for our lives. It's a journey that begins with acknowledging our pain and allowing ourselves to grieve fully and deeply.

When grief turns to depression, it can feel as if we are lost in a sea of darkness, with no shore in sight. Fortunately, we serve a God who is intimately acquainted with grief, who knows what it is to suffer loss. Jesus wept at the tomb of Lazarus, his friend, showing us that it is okay to mourn, to feel the weight of our sorrow.

Along the pathway to healing, we are also called to seek help from others—to lean on our faith community, our friends, and our family for support. It may be beneficial to seek out professional help from a mental health counselor. These special people are wonderful instruments of healing and wholeness in the hands of God. We are called to be open and honest about our struggles, knowing that vulnerability is not a sign of weakness, but a step towards healing.

And as we journey towards healing, we remember that God is in the business of making all things new. He is a God of restoration and redemption, and he can take our deepest pain and turn it into something beautiful. He can bring beauty from ashes, joy from mourning, and hope from despair.

So let us journey towards healing with faith and courage, knowing that God is with us every step of the way. May we trust in His plan for our lives and lean on His strength to carry us through.

And may we emerge from the darkness of depression into the light of His love, whole and healed, ready to embrace the future He has planned for us.

Amen.

# Recapturing the Rhythm of Life

Life has a rhythm, a cadence of routines and seasons that often remain unchanged. Yet, there are interludes when the melody is disrupted; when the familiar notes give way to a discordant symphony of suffering, adversity, or loss. In these times, we find ourselves navigating through uncharted waters, grappling with emotions and experiences that alter us at our core.

As the world around us rushes back to normalcy, we may find ourselves standing on the shore of what once was, hesitant to step forward. The routines resume, but we are different. The pain, the struggle, the questions linger, casting a shadow over the path ahead. How do we re-enter life when the landscape of our hearts and minds has been forever changed?

"When you pass through the waters, I will be with you; and when you pass through the rivers, they will not sweep over you." – Isaiah 43:2. As we step tentatively into the familiar rhythms of life, we may find that our faith beats to a different tune. The melodies of the past, once strong and sure, may now carry a haunting echo of doubt or a bittersweet harmony of resilience. How do we find our place in this new symphony of faith?

Perhaps faith, much like life, is not about returning to the old normal but about embracing a new normalcy. It is about discovering a rhythm that resonates with the depths of our soul, a rhythm that acknowledges the scars of the past while embracing the possibilities

# The Tapestry of Life

of the future. It is about finding beauty in the brokenness, strength in the struggle, and hope in the healing.

The journey of faith is not a sprint but a marathon, a winding path that leads us through valleys of despair and up the mountains of hope. As we navigate the terrain of life after hardship, we are called to embrace the journey ahead with courage and conviction. It is in the moments of uncertainty that our faith is tested and strengthened.

Like a ship navigating through a storm, we must trust in the unseen hands of God that guide us, knowing that even in the darkest of nights, the dawn will break, and the sun will rise again. Our faith may be scarred, but it is also resilient, capable of weathering the fiercest of storms.

As we re-enter life after a period of difficulty, let us do so with open hearts and minds, ready to embrace the beauty of a life transformed by grace. Let us remember that we are not defined by our past but by the possibilities of our future, a future shaped by our faith in God that carries us through the darkest of nights, knowing that joy comes in the morning.

# The Onslaught of Abuse

In the shadowed corners of our lives, abuse casts a long and chilling shadow. Its effects ripple through our souls, leaving us gasping for breath, wondering why the very places meant for love and safety became breeding grounds for pain and betrayal. As followers of Christ, we are not immune to the wounds of abuse. In fact, we may find ourselves grappling even more deeply with its impact, wrestling with questions of faith, justice, and the very nature of God.

In the depths of our suffering, abuse stands as a cruel and heartless oppressor, leaving us gasping for air in a world that seems to have lost its warmth. The wounds of abuse cut deep, tearing at the very fabric of our being, leaving us feeling raw and exposed, as if our souls have been laid bare for all to see.

At the heart of abuse lies a perversion of God's design for relationships. Instead of love, there is manipulation; instead of care, there is cruelty. The deep wounds of abuse pierce not just flesh but the very fabric of our identity, leaving us feeling broken and shattered, as if we are unworthy of love or redemption.

As followers of Christ, we are not shielded from the pain of abuse. Instead, we find ourselves grappling with the weight of our suffering in the shadow of the cross. We wonder, in our darkest moments, where God is in the midst of our pain, why He allows such cruelty to exist in a world that He created out of love.

Yet, in the midst of our pain, we are reminded of the profound truth of the Gospel: that we serve a God who sees our pain, who hears our cries, and who walks with us through the darkest valleys.

# The Tapestry of Life

In Isaiah 53:3, we are reminded that Jesus Himself was "a man of sorrows, acquainted with deepest grief." He understands our pain because He bore it Himself on the cross.

Jesus extends a gentle invitation to those who are weary and burdened, promising rest for our souls. He understands our pain, for He Himself endured unimaginable suffering on the cross, bearing the weight of all our sin and shame.

In our journey towards healing, we are invited to bring our pain to the foot of the cross, where Christ's compassion becomes the balm that soothes our wounds. It is in our brokenness that we find the transformative power of Christ's love, healing us from the inside out, and restoring our sense of dignity and worth.

As we navigate the complexities of abuse, we are called to extend compassion to ourselves. We are reminded that our pain is valid and deserving of empathy, not judgment or condemnation. It is through this act of compassion that we begin to heal, slowly stitching together the tattered pieces of our souls into a beautiful tapestry of resilience and grace.

In the midst of our suffering, let us cling to the promise of Psalm 34:18, that "The Lord is close to the brokenhearted and saves those who are crushed in spirit." Though we may never fully understand the why of our suffering, we can take comfort in the knowledge that God is with us, walking beside us in our pain, and guiding us towards healing and wholeness.

Our pain is not the end of our story. We are reminded that God has preserved us through the suffering and misery because He has a plan and purpose for our lives. Just like Job, we may never understand why the abuse occurred. And just like Job, we must find our answers in the very Person of God. It is only in Him that we can find rest for our souls.

If you are reading this devotional and have survived the onslaught of abuse, both past and present, please know I have prayed for you. I ask that all of us who are reading this devotional take a moment to pray for those who carry the wounds of abuse in their bodies and souls. Some may be experiencing abuse today. Let's pray that God delivers them and ministers healing to them.

# Connections

Life, a tapestry of moments, weaves a story of connection—threads of love, pain, laughter, and tears intertwining to create a masterpiece of shared experience. At its core, life beckons us to connect, to reach beyond ourselves and touch the lives of others; for in connection, we find meaning, purpose, and the very essence of what it means to be human.

Connection is not merely a desire; it is a primal need, ingrained in the fabric of our being by our Creator. From the dawn of creation, God declared, "It is not good for man to be alone" (Gen. 2:18). We are designed for relationships, fashioned to walk this journey of life hand in hand with our fellow travelers.

In a world marked by division and isolation, the call to connect resonates with a deep longing within our souls. Yet, true connection requires more than mere proximity; it demands vulnerability, the willingness to open our hearts and share our lives with others. It is in this vulnerability that we find true connection, for it is in our brokenness that we discover our shared humanity.

Connection is a source of strength, a lifeline in the stormy seas of life. Ecclesiastes reminds us, "Two are better than one, because they have a good return for their labor: If either of them falls down, one can help the other up. But pity anyone who falls and has no one to help them up" (Eccles. 4:9-10). In moments of weakness, connection offers us a shoulder to lean on, a hand to hold, a voice to reassure us that we are not alone.

Connection is also a source of joy, a celebration of shared experiences and mutual understanding. It is in connection that we find laughter sweeter, sorrows shared lighter, and triumphs more meaningful. Connection enriches our lives, infusing each moment with a depth, and richness, that transcends the ordinary.

Most profoundly, connection reflects the heart of God, who exists eternally in perfect communion within the Trinity. As children of God, we are called to mirror this divine connection in our relationships with one another. Jesus exemplified this when He said, "A new command I give you: Love one another. As I have loved you, so you must love one another" (John 13:34-35).

In a society that often values individualism and self-reliance, let us embrace the sacred dance of connection. Let us reach out to one another with open hearts and willing hands, ready to share in the joys and sorrows of life. Let us cultivate relationships that are deep and meaningful, reflecting the love and grace of our Heavenly Father.

As we dance the dance of connection, may we be reminded of the profound truth that we are all interconnected, bound together by the sacred thread of God's love.

# Hope, Faith, and Love

Hope, like a beacon in the night, shines brightly in the human heart. It is enduring, steadfast in the face of adversity, and resilient amidst life's trials. Hope does not stand alone; it is accompanied by its faithful companions: faith and love. Together, these three virtues form a powerful triumvirate that sustains us through the darkest of times and illuminates our path with light and purpose.

Hope whispers in our ear, urging us to treasure each moment, for it is a gift from God. Hope gives us the capacity to appreciate life in all its beauty and complexity. It is the belief that tomorrow can be better than today, that there is always a reason to keep going, to keep striving.

Faith, on the other hand, grants us the understanding that life is a gift from God, filled with meaning and purpose. It is the assurance that we are never alone, that there is a divine plan unfolding even in the midst of chaos and confusion.

Love, perhaps the most potent of the three, is the catalyst that propels us out of our self-centeredness and preoccupation with our own difficulties. Love calls us to action, to reach out beyond ourselves, and touch the lives of others with kindness and compassion. It is active, persistent, and transformative. Love has the power to heal the most wounded of souls, to mend broken hearts, and to restore hope where it has been lost.

Together, hope, faith, and love create a symphony of grace and beauty, harmonizing to orchestrate healing and wholeness in our lives. They remind us that life is a gift, a precious tapestry woven

# The Tapestry of Life

with threads of joy and sorrow; victory and defeat. Each moment is a brushstroke, painting a picture of our journey towards a greater understanding of ourselves and the world around us.

When hope, faith, and love converge, they create a space where healing and wholeness can be found. Miracles happen, hearts are mended, dreams are realized, and lives are transformed. They remind us that each one of us has the capacity to be an instrument of hope, a beacon of light in a world that can sometimes seem dark and cold. They are the pillars of our existence; the foundation upon which we build our future aspirations.

So, have faith, dear friend, that God is at work in your life, fashioning all things for your good and His glory. You are not insignificant; you matter. Your presence, your actions, and your love can make a difference in someone's life today.

Let us, then, be bearers of hope, agents of faith, and ambassadors of love. Let us shine brightly in the darkness, knowing that our light, however small, can dispel the shadows and bring warmth to the coldest of hearts. May we illuminate the path for others and show them that, no matter how dark the night may seem, the dawn will always break, bringing with it a new day filled with endless possibilities

# Practicing Gentleness

The most influential, profoundly wise, and discerning people in my life have all been gentle people. It takes a special strength to cultivate and live from a place of gentleness. Gentleness is a fruit of the Spirit. Gentleness is healing. Gentle people are often peacemakers. Gentle people serve others, not themselves.

In a world often marked by conflict and discord, the value of gentleness calls to us as a place of refuge and shelter, a safe harbor from a harsh and tempestuous world. Gentle people provide these safe spaces for us. They are a welcome respite from the noise and din of a world that sometimes seems overwhelming.

When we think of those who have deeply influenced us, it is often the gentle ones who leave the most enduring legacy. Their gentleness is not a sign of weakness but of profound resilience and character. These are men and women who have learned to trust in God when the gales of adversity howl around them.

Gentleness, as described in the Bible, is a fruit of the Spirit, a quality that reflects the nature of God Himself. When we cultivate gentleness in our lives, we align ourselves with a higher purpose and a deeper understanding of what it means to love others. Gentleness is not merely a passive trait; it is an active choice to respond to life's challenges with grace and kindness. Gentle people are often peacemakers, seeking to mend relationships and bridge divides. They speak with a special wisdom when the headwinds of difficulty buffet us.

In moments of tension and conflict, gentleness has the power to change the course of events. Instead of escalating a situation, gentleness can lead us to peaceful resolutions and harmonious outcomes. They calm frayed nerves and prevent the intensity of the moment from becoming something ugly. It is a reminder that being strong does not mean being harsh or abrasive; true strength lies in the ability to remain gentle even in the face of adversity.

Practicing gentleness is not always easy, especially in a world that often values assertiveness and aggression. Yet, the impact of gentleness is profound, both in our own lives and in the lives of those around us. It is a reminder that kindness and compassion can go a long way in healing wounds and bringing about positive change.

Today, as you go about your day, I encourage you to reflect on the fruit of gentleness. Look for opportunities to practice gentleness in your interactions with others. Whether it is a gentle word of encouragement or a kind gesture of support, your acts of gentleness can make a difference in the world around you.

# Wounded by Words

In the tapestry of life, our hearts are delicate threads, easily snagged and torn by the sharp words of others. In the quiet of our hearts, we shelter the tender places, the parts of us easily wounded by the careless words of people—often people who do not know us—yet they believe they have the right or authority to harm with words. It's a pain that cuts deep, leaving invisible scars that linger long after the words have faded into silence.

When someone speaks unkindly of us, it's as if they reach into the very core of our being, touching a raw nerve that sends waves of hurt and confusion through our souls. It's a sensation akin to a sharp knife slicing through the fabric of our self, our personhood, leaving behind a tattered and fragile sense of worth. The words hang in the air, heavy and suffocating, like a dense fog that obscures our vision and clouds our thoughts.

It's easy to feel alone, as if no one else could possibly understand the depth of our pain. Yet, we are not alone. The One who knit us together in our mother's womb, who knows every hair on our head, also knows the hurt in our hearts. He sees every tear we shed, and He longs to comfort us in our distress. He sees beyond the hurtful words to the beauty and potential that lie within us, waiting to be revealed.

It's natural to want to lash out in anger or retreat into ourselves in shame when faced with hurtful words. But there is another way—a way of grace and forgiveness. Just as we have been forgiven, so too are we called to forgive those who have spoken ill of us. It's a difficult path to walk, but one that leads to healing and freedom.

But just as a skilled artisan can mend a broken vase, so too can God mend our broken hearts. He is the master craftsman, gently picking up the pieces of our shattered souls, and fashioning them back together with His love and grace. In His hands, our brokenness becomes a thing of beauty, a testament to His power to heal and restore.

Ultimately, we can take comfort in knowing that the hurtful words of others do not define us. Our true worth comes from God alone, and nothing that anyone else says can change that. As we rest in this truth, we can find the strength to forgive those who have hurt us and to move forward with grace and dignity.

So, if you find yourself wounded by the words of others, take heart. You are not alone, and this pain will not last forever. Allow God to heal your hurts and to fill you with His peace. And remember, you are cherished, valued, and deeply loved beyond all measure—just as you are. You are His beloved child, and no words spoken against you can ever change that.

# WE ARE REVELATORS OF GOD

In the intricate tapestry of life, God uses us as threads to weave His story of love, grace, and redemption. Each of us is a unique expression of His creativity, crafted with purpose and intentionality. Through us, God reveals different facets of His character, showing the world His love, mercy, and power.

God's revelation through us is not limited to our strengths or abilities. In fact, He often chooses to reveal Himself through our weaknesses and imperfections. In 2 Corinthians 12:9, Paul writes, "But he said to me, 'My grace is sufficient for you, for my power is made perfect in weakness.'" God's strength is made evident in our weaknesses, demonstrating His ability to work through us despite our limitations.

Think of a broken pot that still holds water. Despite its imperfection, it serves its purpose. Similarly, God uses our brokenness to reveal His healing and restoring power. In our vulnerability, His strength shines through, showing others that He is the ultimate source of hope and restoration.

God also reveals Himself through our actions and attitudes. When we show love to those who are difficult to love, we reflect God's unconditional love. When we extend forgiveness to those who have wronged us, we mirror God's forgiveness. Our lives become a living testimony to God's transformative power, drawing others to Him.

God uses our stories to reveal His faithfulness. As we share our testimonies of how God has worked in our lives, we become living epistles, testifying to His goodness and faithfulness. Our stories become a source of hope to those who are struggling, showing them that God is still in the business of changing lives.

God also reveals Himself through the community of believers. In John 13:35, Jesus says, "By this everyone will know that you are my disciples if you love one another." When we love one another, pray for one another, encourage one another, and support one another despite our differences, we demonstrate God's inclusive love that transcends all boundaries.

As we surrender ourselves to God's will, He uses us as instruments of His grace and love, revealing Himself to a world that is desperate for hope and meaning. Let us be willing vessels, allowing God to use us to reveal His beauty and majesty to the world around us.

# The Solace of
# Silent Ministry

Imagine standing at the edge of a vast, turbulent sea; its waves crashing relentlessly against the shore. You watch as a friend navigates a storm in their life; the waves of sorrow and despair threatening to overwhelm them. You long to offer them a lifeboat of words, to rescue them with your wisdom and comfort. But as you reach out, you find yourself at a loss, your words swept away by the howling wind. In such a desperate situation, it's natural to feel powerless, to question the adequacy of your support.

As you sit together, you become aware of the rawness of their pain, the heaviness of their heart. You feel the weight of their burden as if it were your own, and in that shared moment, a bond is forged that transcends words. It is a sacred communion of souls; a reminder that love is not always spoken but often felt in the silence.

In the depths of your friend's sorrow, you catch a glimpse of their innermost thoughts and feelings. You see their fear, their uncertainty, and their longing for comfort. You ache to ease their pain, to erase the hurt etched upon their face. Yet, you know that some wounds can only heal with time, and so you offer the only balm you have—your unwavering presence.

In the silence, you feel a myriad of emotions—sadness, empathy, and a deep sense of connection. You are reminded of your own struggles, your own moments of pain and sorrow. But you are not focused on yourself; rather, you are focused on your friend by offering them the support and comfort they need.

It is often in the silence, in the simple act of being present, that the deepest comfort is found. Like a sturdy lighthouse standing firm amidst the storm, your presence steadies their soul, guiding your friend through the darkness.

We sometimes encounter situations where family and friends are going through such intense suffering, pain, and loss, that our hearts wither from the intensity of their hurt. We cannot fix, mend, alleviate, or provide a remedy for their pain. We can only be…be with them and for them. Even the Bible says there are times when "weeping with those who weep" is the best, most appropriate way we can express our love, care, and support.

Ask God to help you be present with them, offering grace, and existing with them in the midst of their adversity. Sit with them in silence, providing them with the reassurance that they are not alone. Your quiet understanding may be the balm that ministers a measure of comfort to their troubled soul.

Please remember, it is God Who makes us adequate for ministry. Trust that God will give you the grace you need to minister to your loved one. Ask God to give you the wisdom to know when to speak and when to simply be there; a silent witness to their pain. May you be used as instruments of love, grace, and healing in the lives of those you hold dear.

# Beautiful People

In a world that often seeks to hide its scars, there is a profound beauty in those who wear their wounds with grace. Elisabeth Kübler-Ross captured this truth when she said, "The most beautiful people we have known are those who have known defeat, known suffering, known struggle, known loss, and have found their way out of the depths." (Ross, *Death:* 1975)

The beauty of resilience is not found in flawless perfection but in the journey through imperfection. It is in the moments of darkness that light shines brightest. Those who have faced defeat and emerged stronger are not defined by their trials but by their resilience in overcoming them.

Suffering and struggle have a way of shaping us, molding us into compassionate beings who understand the depth of human experience. It is through our own pain that we can truly empathize with the pain of others. This empathy leads to compassion, a deep-seated concern for the well-being of others that is born out of our own struggles.

Loss, perhaps more than anything else, has the power to transform us. The absence left behind by a loved one can be overwhelming, but it is in this absence that we discover the depth of our love. It is in the empty spaces that we learn to cherish the memories and hold onto the love that remains.

Our faith teaches us that our struggles are not in vain. They are opportunities for God to work in us and through us, shaping us into vessels of His grace and love. In our moments of defeat, we are reminded of our need for a Savior. In our suffering, we find comfort in the arms of our loving God. In our struggles, we discover the strength that comes from relying on His power. And in our losses, we experience the hope of a future reunion in heaven.

It is through these experiences that we develop an appreciation, a sensitivity, and an understanding of life that fills us with compassion, gentleness, and a deep loving concern. Our struggles cultivate in us a heart that mirrors the heart of Christ, a heart that beats with love for the broken and the hurting.

Beautiful people do not just happen. They are forged in the fires of life's challenges and emerge as shining examples of resilience and grace. They are the ones who, despite their scars, radiate love and compassion, offering hope to those around them.

As we navigate our own journeys, let us remember that beauty is not found in perfection but in the courage to embrace our imperfections. Let us embrace our defeats, our sufferings, our struggles, and our losses, knowing that they are not the end of our story but the beginning of a beautiful transformation. May we emerge from the depths of our trials as beautiful testimonies to God's grace and faithfulness, shining brightly for all to see.

# Bumping into Absences

In the tapestry of life, God weaves our stories with the threads of love, joy, and shared moments. Yet, there are moments when we bump into the absences left behind by those who have departed from this earthly journey. These absences are like holes in our tapestry, reminding us of the loved ones who once stood beside us; their presence now a cherished memory.

As Christians, we are not immune to the pain of loss. Even though we have the hope of eternity with Christ, the pain of separation in this life is very real. We are reminded in Ecclesiastes 3:1-4 that there is a time for everything, including a time to mourn. When we bump into the absences left behind by our loved ones, we are allowed to mourn, to grieve the loss of their physical presence in our lives.

Grief is a journey that leads us through a landscape of emotions, sometimes gentle as a whisper and other times fierce as a storm. When we bump into these absences, we are confronted with the reality of loss, a void that cannot be filled by anyone or anything else. It's in these moments that we feel the weight of our sorrow, the ache of missing someone deeply ingrained in our hearts.

As we navigate through the labyrinth of grief, we find ourselves wrestling with a myriad of emotions. There's sadness, of course, a deep and profound sadness that seems to engulf us at times. There's also anger, a righteous anger at the unfairness of it all, the feeling that life has dealt us a cruel hand. And then there's the emptiness, a hollow feeling in the pit of our stomachs, a sense of longing for the one we have lost.

But amidst the pain and the sorrow, there is also grace and hope. For in the midst of our grief, we are reminded of the promise of resurrection and reunion in Christ. We are reminded that death does not have the final say, that through Christ, we have the hope of eternal life

We are reminded of the love that binds us to those we have lost. We are reminded of the moments we shared, the laughter, the tears, the joy, and the sorrow. We are reminded that love is eternal, that it transcends the boundaries of time and space.

Memories become our lifeline, a way to keep the flame of love burning bright in our hearts. We cherish the moments we shared, holding onto them like precious treasures. And in those moments, we find comfort, a balm for our wounded souls.

Grief is not a journey that we walk alone. God is with us every step of the way, as are our friends and family. Along the way, we encounter others who have walked this path before us, their presence a source of comfort in the darkness.

They remind us of that grief, though painful, is also a testament to the love we shared with those we have lost.

So, as we bump into the absences left behind by our loved ones, let us remember that grief is a journey of love. It is a journey that honors the love we shared, a journey that reminds us of the depth of our emotions. And in the end, it is a journey that leads us to a place of healing, a place where love reigns supreme, and where absences are filled with the grace of memories.

# Journeying Through the Darkness

In the depths of despair, where shadows loom large and hope seems but a distant memory, there lies a journey we all face…we all must embark upon. It is a journey through the darkness, struggling to emerge from a dank desolation that drags us down into the cloying grasp of despondency. It's a journey of digging deep within oneself to get up and move through this dark place.

When the darkness of hell threatens to overwhelm you…keep walking. Don't stop. Pray that God gives you strength to endure.

Imagine a vast, cavernous tunnel; its walls slick with the dampness of tears shed in solitude. You stand at its entrance, surrounded by the echoes of your own despair. The weight of the world bears down upon your shoulders, threatening to crush your spirit beneath its heavy burden. As you move through the unknown and uncertainty, you are enveloped by the echoes of our own brokenness. And so, you begin again…you begin to walk through the darkness.

You confront the demons of your past, those fears and doubts that have held you captive for so long. With each memory uncovered, you find healing and closure, laying to rest the ghosts that have haunted your soul. You persevere through the guilt and pain of present failings…recent wounds…some you have inflicted unintentionally on yourself. But you keep walking…moving forward… one step at a time.

# The Tapestry of Life

The journey is not without its challenges. There are moments when the darkness threatens to overwhelm you, when the weight of your past feels too heavy to bear. In those moments, you must reach deep within yourself, finding strength in the knowledge that you are not alone…finding strength in the knowledge that God is with us. Above us, the world continues on, bathed in the light of God's love. His creation sings His praises, a reminder that He is always near, even in our darkest hour. The sun rises and sets, a testament to His faithfulness and the promise of a new day.

You stand exhausted, your body bruised and weary, but your spirit renewed. You have emerged from the darkness, not unscathed, but stronger and more resilient than before, forgiven and redeemed. You have faced your fears and overcome them, digging deep within yourself to find the Light of God that has guided you to this moment.

As you stand in the light of a new dawn, take a moment to reflect on your journey. You have proven to yourself that, with God's enablement, you are capable of great strength and resilience, that even in the darkest of times, there is always a flicker of hope. Embrace this newfound strength, and let it help you move forward into a future filled with possibility and promise.

If you are in a dark place today and you are reading this devotional, please know I have prayed for you. May God Himself be your encouragement, today and always.

And always remember that God is with us. He has never left us or forsaken us. You are greatly loved.

# Tending to Our Souls

Our souls are like a garden, often overrun by the weeds of worry and the thorns of turmoil. In the busyness of life, it's easy to neglect this sacred space, allowing the noise of the world to drown out the gentle whisper of our hearts. Yet, beneath the surface, there lies a wellspring of peace, a quiet refuge where we can find solace amidst life's storms.

Imagine this garden, untended and overgrown, with vines of anxiety creeping up the walls of our hearts and thorns of fear scratching at the windows of our souls. In the midst of this chaos, it's hard to imagine that peace could ever take root and flourish. And yet, if we take the time to clear away the clutter, to pull up the weeds, and prune back the thorns, we will find that peace is not far off—it's been waiting for us all along.

Just as a gardener tends to his garden, so too must we tend to our souls. We must cultivate a spirit of peace, watering it with prayer, and nourishing it with the promises of God's Word. We must uproot the weeds of worry and fear, replacing them with the seeds of faith and trust. And we must prune back the thorns of turmoil, allowing the light of God's love to shine into the darkest corners of our hearts.

In the stillness of this sacred space, we are reminded that peace is not the absence of noise but the presence of God. Like a skilled composer, God orchestrates the symphony of our lives, weaving together the highs and lows, the joys and sorrows, into a harmonious whole. He knows the melody of our hearts, and He longs to lead us into a place of rest and restoration.

## The Tapestry of Life

Psalm 46 paints a vivid picture of God as our fortress, our refuge in times of trouble. It is in the shadow of His wings that we find shelter from the storm, a place of safety and security amidst life's uncertainties. As we quiet our souls before Him, we find that His peace surpasses all understanding, filling us with a sense of calm and tranquility that cannot be shaken by the trials of this world.

So, my dear friend, if your soul is disquieted today, take heart. The peace you seek is closer than you think. It is within you, waiting to be uncovered, waiting to be embraced. May you find rest in the quiet sanctuary of your soul, and may the peace of God, which surpasses all understanding, guard your heart and mind in Christ Jesus.

# Battered by Betrayal

Betrayal is a jagged crack in the foundation of trust we've painstakingly built, a fracture that sends tremors of hurt and disbelief through the very core of our being. It's like standing on solid ground one moment, only to find ourselves freefalling into a void of confusion and pain the next.

Imagine the heart as a fragile glass sculpture, each friendship a delicate, hand-blown piece intricately connected to the whole. Betrayal shatters that sculpture, leaving us to pick up the pieces, our hands bleeding from the sharp edges of broken trust.

Betrayal stings deeply, but when compounded by the added hurt of friends remaining loyal to the one who betrayed us, the pain can feel unbearable. It's a unique kind of heartache, a sense of betrayal upon betrayal, a feeling of abandonment by those we thought were on our side. The pain of compounded betrayal lingers like the bitter taste of bile in the back of our throat, leaving a heaviness in our chest that makes it hard to breathe.

When friends choose to stay connected with the one who has hurt us, it can feel like a second betrayal. We may wonder if our friendships were ever genuine; if our pain even matters to those around us. We might question the loyalty and authenticity of these relationships, feeling a sense of isolation and abandonment. It's the feeling of being invisible, of our pain being dismissed or ignored. It's the ache of a wound that refuses to heal, a constant reminder of our vulnerability.

The hurt cuts deep.

We may grapple with feelings of rejection, unworthiness, and deep sadness. We may struggle with anger, wondering why our friends can't see the pain that we're going through. We may even be tempted to withdraw, to close ourselves off from others to protect ourselves from further hurt.

But, as is often the case, we find the seeds of hope germinating in the midst of the pain. We find our comfort in knowing that we are not alone in our suffering. Jesus, too, experienced betrayal by those closest to Him. He understands the pain of being abandoned and rejected by friends. He knows what it's like to feel the sting of betrayal, and He offers us His comfort and understanding.

We can also find strength in the knowledge that our worth is not determined by the actions of others. Our value is not contingent on whether or not others choose to stand by us. We are deeply loved and cherished by a God who will never abandon us, who will never betray us.

As we navigate the pain of betrayal and the added hurt of friends remaining loyal to the one who hurt us, let us turn to God for comfort and strength. Let us lean on Him in our moments of weakness, knowing that He is with us, offering us His love and grace. And let us remember that, even in our darkest moments, we are never alone. God is with us, holding us in His embrace, whispering words of love and healing over our brokenness. And in His time, He will turn our pain into something beautiful, a testimony to His faithfulness and our resilience.

# Work as Worship

In the tapestry of life, our work is a thread—a strand of purpose woven into the fabric of existence. From the moment we rise until we rest our heads, our days are filled with tasks, responsibilities, and obligations. But what if we were to view these moments not as mere duties, but as opportunities for worship?

Consider the artisan, hands deftly crafting a piece of furniture. Each stroke of the chisel, each smooth pass of sandpaper, is an act of creation, a reflection of the Divine Craftsman who formed us from the dust of the earth. In the workshop, amidst the scent of wood shavings and the sound of a hammer on nail, there is a sacredness—a recognition that our work is a partnership with the Creator.

Or think of the nurse, tending to the sick and the suffering with compassion and care. In her ministrations, she embodies the love and healing touch of the Divine Physician, bringing comfort to the hurting and hope to the despairing. Her work is a form of worship, a way of offering gentle, skilled support to those in need.

Many of our family members are farmers, tilling the soil and sowing seeds with hands weathered and worn. In his labor, he finds communion with the One who provides seed for the sower and bread for the eater, recognizing that his work is part of a larger cycle of growth and sustenance.

Even the most ordinary tasks can be infused with meaning and purpose. The cashier who smiles and greets each customer, the bus driver who safely transports passengers to their destinations, and the office worker who diligently completes her tasks—all are engaged in acts of worship, honoring the sacredness of their work and the dignity of those they serve. The janitor who sweeps the floors, the accountant who balances the books, and the teacher who imparts knowledge—they are all part of a symphony of work; each note contributing to the melody of creation.

So let us approach each day with a sense of reverence and gratitude, knowing that our work is not just a means to an end but also a way in which we honor God with the calling He has placed on our lives. Let us approach each day with a sense of purpose and intentionality, knowing that our effort is not in vain but is part of a larger, cosmic narrative. May we see our tasks not as burdens to be borne but as gifts to be embraced, offering them up as incense rising to the heavens, to the glory of God.

# The Wilderness of Uncertainty

In the vast expanse of life's journey, there are moments when the path ahead seems shrouded in an impenetrable mist, and we find ourselves wandering in a wilderness of uncertainty. The feeling of being lost and alone can weigh heavily on our hearts, casting a shadow over our thoughts and emotions. In the recesses of the soul's darkest caverns, where shadows dance and whispers echo, there lies a place untouched by the light of day.

It is a place of solitude, where the heart's cries are muffled by the weight of despair…a place where the very air seems heavy with the absence of hope, and the stars above offer no guidance. In these moments of profound isolation, it is easy to believe that we are adrift in an ocean of emptiness, with no shore in sight, no lighthouse to guide our way. We may feel like the psalmist in Psalm 88:14, who cries out, "Why, Lord, do you reject me and hide your face from me?" Again, in verse 18, "You have taken from me friend and neighbor—darkness is my closest friend."

It is easy to believe that we are truly alone in the world, abandoned by those we love, and forsaken by the heavens. The silence that surrounds us can be deafening, drowning out the whispers of hope and faith that once filled our hearts.

Yet, even in the midst of this darkness, there is a light that shines, a light that cannot be extinguished. It is the light of God's love, a love that knows no bounds and reaches into the deepest recesses of our souls. It is a love that is as constant as the northern star, guiding us through the darkest nights and the most treacherous terrain. God's love is a love that transcends all barriers and reaches into the innermost parts of our souls. It is a love that brings warmth to our coldest nights and hope to our darkest days.

In Isaiah 43:2, God says, "When you pass through the waters, I will be with you; and when you pass through the rivers, they will not sweep over you. When you walk through the fire, you will not be burned; the flames will not set you ablaze." These words are a reminder that God's love is the radiance of hope in our darkest moments, a light that leads us out of the wilderness and into the promised land.

When we feel lost and alone, we can turn to God in prayer, knowing that He hears our cries and understands our pain. In Psalm 34:17, David writes, "The righteous cry out, and the Lord hears them; he delivers them from all their troubles." God is not a distant deity, but a loving Father who longs to comfort us in our times of need.

So, as you journey through the wilderness of life, remember that you are never truly alone. God's love is a light in the darkness, a sunbeam of hope that shines brightly, guiding you, comforting you, and giving you the strength to carry on. Trust in His love, and you will find your way out of the wilderness, into the light of His presence.

# Overcoming Obstacles to Growth

Change and growth are like the rhythm of a heart beating with the promise of transformation and renewal in our Christian journey. Yet, despite their beauty and purpose, many of us find ourselves resisting these very elements that are meant to draw us closer to God and deepen our faith. Understanding these resistances can help us embrace the transformative work God wants to do in our lives more fully.

Fear often stands as a formidable barrier to change and growth. Stepping into the unknown, leaving behind the familiar and comfortable, can be daunting. We naturally crave security and stability, fearing the loss of control and the uncertainty of the future. This fear can paralyze us, keeping us from taking the steps necessary to grow in our faith.

Complacency, too, can hinder our spiritual journey. It's easy to settle into a routine, content with where we are spiritually. We may resist anything that challenges us to move beyond our current level of maturity, fearing that change will disrupt the comfort of our routines and traditions. This complacency can blind us to the deeper work God wants to do in our lives, stifling our spiritual growth.

Pride, with its deceptive allure, can also lead us astray. We may believe that we have all the answers, that we don't need to change or grow any further. This attitude of self-sufficiency can prevent us from seeking God's guidance and relying on His strength to transform us. Pride blinds us to our need for change and growth, leading to stagnation in our spiritual lives.

Insecurity, too, plays a role in our resistance to change and growth. We may doubt our abilities or feel unworthy of God's love and grace. This insecurity can cause us to resist stepping out in faith or embracing new opportunities for growth. We may fear failure or rejection, choosing to stay within our comfort zones rather than taking risks for God.

To overcome these barriers, we must surrender our fears, complacency, pride, and insecurities to God. We must trust that He has a plan for our lives and that His plan is for our good. We must be willing to step out in faith, even when it is uncomfortable or frightening, trusting that God is leading us into a deeper relationship with Him. As we surrender and trust, we will find that God is faithful to transform us, leading us into a life of greater abundance and joy.

# God: Our Dwelling Place

Psalm 90:1 begins with a profound declaration: "Lord, you have been our dwelling place throughout all generations." These words, penned by Moses, reflect a deep truth about our relationship with God. They remind us that God is not merely a temporary shelter but a timeless dwelling place, a constant refuge for every generation.

In the ever-changing landscape of life, where uncertainties loom large and the future remains unknown, we find great comfort and security in knowing that God is our dwelling place. He is not confined by time or limited by circumstances. He transcends all generations, offering His presence as a source of strength, acceptance, and belonging.

As we navigate the challenges of our day-to-day lives, it's easy to seek refuge in temporary comforts—material possessions, human relationships, or personal achievements. While these may offer temporary relief, they fail to provide the lasting peace and security that our souls crave. They are but fleeting shelters in the midst of life's storms.

God, however, offers us something far greater. He invites us to dwell in His presence, to find our refuge in Him alone. In Him, we find a safe haven, a place of rest for our weary souls. He is our shelter in times of trouble, our fortress in the face of adversity.

When we make God our dwelling place, we acknowledge our dependence on Him. We recognize that apart from Him, we are vulnerable and exposed. But in Him, we find strength and protection.

He becomes our constant companion, walking with us through every season of life.

This truth is not just for us but for all generations. From the beginning of time until the end of the age, God remains the same. His love endures forever; His faithfulness never wavers. As we look back at the faithfulness of God in the lives of those who have gone before us, we are encouraged to trust Him with our own lives.

Today, let us take refuge in the timeless dwelling place of God. Let us rest in His presence, knowing that He is our shelter in the storm. May we find peace in His promises and strength in His unfailing love. And may we, like Moses, declare with confidence, "Lord, you have been our dwelling place throughout all generations."

# HOPE FOR HEALING

In life, we often face moments of deep pain and sorrow, moments where our wounds seem too deep to heal, and the pain too real to bear. These wounds can be physical, emotional, or spiritual, and they leave us feeling broken and helpless. It can be easy to lose hope, to feel like the pain will never go away, and that the wounds will never heal. However, as followers of Christ, we are called to a different response.

The lyrics, "These wounds won't seem to heal, this pain is just too real, there's just too much that time cannot erase," [KS9] ( Evanescence. "My Immortal." Track 4 on *Fallen*. Wind-up Records, 2003.) echo the sentiments of many who are struggling with pain and suffering. It can be difficult to see beyond the pain, to believe that there is hope for healing, and that there is a purpose for our suffering. However, as Christians, we are called to trust in God's plan for our lives, even when we cannot see the way forward.

As Christians, we believe in a God who understands our pain and suffering, a God who himself endured unimaginable suffering for our sake. One of the most profound examples of finding healing in unhealed wounds is found in the life of Jesus. On the cross, Jesus experienced the ultimate pain and suffering, both physically and emotionally. His wounds were deep, and his pain was real. Yet, through his suffering, Jesus brought about the ultimate healing for all of humanity. His wounds became a source of healing and redemption for us all.

As followers of Christ, we are called to follow His example, to find healing in our own wounds, and to use our pain to bring about healing and redemption in the world around us. This is not an easy task, and it requires us to trust in God's plan for our lives, even when we cannot see the way forward. It requires us to have faith that God can use our suffering for good, and that He can bring about healing in ways that we cannot imagine.

In the book of Isaiah, we are reminded that God is able to bring about healing in the most unlikely of ways. Isaiah 53:5 says, "But He was pierced for our transgressions, He was crushed for our iniquities; the punishment that brought us peace was on Him, and by His wounds we are healed." This verse reminds us that God is able to bring about healing and redemption through our suffering, just as He did through the suffering of Jesus.

As we navigate our own pain and suffering, let us remember that God is with us, that He understands our pain, and that He is able to bring about healing in ways that we cannot imagine. Let us trust in His plan for our lives and let us use our own wounds as a source of healing and redemption in the world around us.

# The Pain of Being Misunderstood

There is an extraordinarily desolate place that some of us will pass through during our lifetimes. In the silence of the heart, there's a loneliness that comes when it seems no one truly understands you, not even those closest to you. It's a profound ache, a feeling of being adrift in a sea of unspoken thoughts and unseen emotions. You long for someone to grasp the depth of your struggles, to see beyond the surface of your smiles, and understand the turmoil within.

The pain of being misunderstood cuts deep. It's a feeling of isolation, of being trapped in your own mind with no escape. You question yourself, wondering if you are too complex, too different, or if others simply lack the empathy to truly see the intricacies of your heart...to truly see you.

In these moments, you may find yourself withdrawing, building walls, and erecting barriers around your heart to protect yourself from further hurt. This is not done out of malice, but out of a deep-seated need to protect ourselves from further hurt. You may even question the value of your own voice, wondering if it's worth sharing your thoughts and feelings if no one will truly understand.

This introspection leads you to confront your deepest insecurities and vulnerabilities. You realize that the longing for understanding stems from a fundamental need for connection and validation. The fear of not being understood speaks to a fear of rejection and abandonment, of being left alone with your thoughts and emotions adrift in the sea of you own mind.

This is a profoundly lonely, dark, and painful place in which to exist. You long for someone to plunge into the depths of your soul, and to unravel the tangled web of your thoughts and emotions. You crave understanding, not just in words but in the unspoken language of the heart. It is a feeling of isolation, of being marooned on an island of your own making, with no bridge to connect you to the shores of others' understanding.

But in the midst of this solitude, there is a flicker of hope—a tiny ember that refuses to be extinguished. It is the knowledge that you are not truly alone, that there are others who, though they may not fully grasp the intricacies of your being, are willing to listen, to empathize, and to try to understand. It is the belief that there is a God Who sees you, Who knows you, and Who understands you completely.

God sees us in our entirety. He knows the depths of our hearts, and He understands our every thought. In Psalm 139:1-3, David writes, "O Lord, you have searched me and known me! You know when I sit down and when I rise up; you discern my thoughts from afar. You search out my path and my lying down and are acquainted with all my ways."

We can turn to God in prayer, laying bare our hearts before Him. He is the One Who truly understands us, Who sees us for who we are, and loves us unconditionally. We can also take comfort in the knowledge that Jesus Himself experienced the pain of being misunderstood. He understands our struggles and walks alongside us in our journey.

As we navigate the complexities of feeling misunderstood, let us also extend grace to ourselves. It's okay to feel hurt, to grieve the lack of understanding from others. Our feelings are valid, and it's important to acknowledge them without judgment.

## The Pain of Being Misunderstood

Know that your longing for understanding is not in vain, that your yearning for connection is shared by many. And remember that, in opening yourself up to others and to God, in sharing your thoughts and feelings with vulnerability and authenticity, you create the possibility for true connection, for an understanding that transcends words and bridges the gap between hearts.

# God's Whispers in the Wind

As Christians, we often find spiritual truths reflected in the natural world around us. In the tapestry of creation, one of the most intriguing elements of nature is the wind; a force that is invisible yet powerful, gentle yet mighty. Throughout the Bible, the wind is used as a metaphor for the presence and work of God in our lives.

In the book of Genesis, we read that the Spirit of God was hovering over the waters at the creation of the world. This image of the Spirit as a gentle wind, moving over the face of the deep, speaks to us of God's creative power and His constant presence in the world. Just as the wind brings life and movement to the waters as God spoke planet Earth into existence, so too does the Spirit bring life and renewal to our souls today.

In the New Testament, Jesus compares the work of the Spirit to the wind, saying, "The wind blows wherever it pleases. You hear its sound, but you cannot tell where it comes from or where it is going. So, it is with everyone born of the Spirit" (John 3:8). This reminds us that the Spirit of God is not bound by our human understanding or control but moves freely and mysteriously, bringing about God's purposes in our lives.

The wind also serves as a reminder of God's sovereignty and power. In the Old Testament, we read of God using the wind to part the waters of the Red Sea, allowing the Israelites to escape from

Egypt. This miraculous event demonstrates God's ability to overcome any obstacle and deliver His people from bondage.

Furthermore, the wind can be a source of comfort and encouragement. In the book of Job, we find Job in misery with suffering and questioning God's purposes. In response, God speaks to Job out of the whirlwind, reminding him of His power and wisdom. While we may not always understand God's ways, we can take comfort in the knowledge that He is in control and working all things for our good (Romans 8:28).

Finally, the wind can be a symbol of change and transformation. Just as the wind can reshape the landscape, so too can the Spirit of God transform our hearts and lives. Sometimes, this process occurs gradually, over many years, much like sand dunes that are formed or rocks that are sculpted by a persistent wind. As we yield to the gentle whisper of God's voice, we can be transformed into the image of Christ, reflecting His love and grace to the world around us.

A warm, sunny, and windy day like we experienced yesterday along the Ohio River has much to teach us. The wind serves as a powerful metaphor for the presence and work of God in our lives. The wind is unseen yet felt. So, too, is God's Spirit working in and through us, guiding, comforting, and transforming us into His likeness. May we always be sensitive to the whisper of God in the wind, and may it lead us closer to Him each day.

# Moments of Wonder

When was the last time you experienced wonder? Not just a passing moment of surprise or awe, but a deep, soul-stirring sense of marvel at the world around you? Perhaps it was when you witnessed a stunning sunset painting the sky with hues of gold and pink, or when you stood beneath a canopy of stars, feeling small yet connected to something vast and mysterious. Maybe it was the first time you held a newborn baby, or when you stumbled upon a hidden gem of a book that spoke to your heart in unexpected ways.

In our fast-paced world, filled with distractions and noise, it's easy to overlook the moments of wonder that pepper our days. We rush from one task to the next, consumed by our thoughts and worries, and fail to see the beauty and magic that surrounds us. But wonder is not something reserved for special occasions or grand adventures; it is present in the everyday moments, waiting to be noticed and embraced.

The poet Mary Oliver once wrote, "Instructions for living a life: Pay attention. Be astonished. Tell about it." [KS10] (Oliver, Mary. *Red Bird*. Boston: Beacon Press, 2008.) These words serve as a gentle reminder to slow down, to open our eyes and hearts to the world around us, and to allow ourselves to be astonished by the beauty and complexity of life.

So, when was the last time you experienced wonder? Maybe it was this morning, when you saw a passage of scripture in a new light, or when you savored the first sip of your morning coffee. Perhaps it was yesterday, when you took a walk outside, felt the sun on your face, and the wind in your hair. Or maybe it was just now, as you read these words, and reflected on the moments of wonder in your own life.

As we go about our days, let us not forget to seek out wonder in the everyday. Let us pause to admire the delicate beauty of a flower, to listen to the nighttime chorus singing the song of life, and to marvel at the ingenuity of the human mind. And let us be grateful for these moments of wonder, for they remind us of the extraordinary nature of the world we inhabit, the gift of being alive, and that we are loved by our Creator.

# Living with Eternity in View

In the busyness of our daily lives, it's easy to get caught up in the here and now, focusing on our immediate needs and desires. But what if we shifted our perspective and began to live with eternity in view? What if we lived each day with the awareness that our time on this earth is just a small part of our eternal journey?

Living with eternity in view is about recognizing that our actions and choices here on earth have eternal significance. It's about living in a way that honors God and reflects His love and grace to those around us. It's about investing in things that will last beyond this life—things like love, kindness, and faith.

When we live with eternity in view, our priorities shift. We no longer chase after fleeting pleasures, or material possessions, but seek to build a legacy of faith and love. We understand that our true treasure is stored up in heaven, where moth and rust cannot destroy.

Living with eternity in view also changes how we view suffering and hardship. Instead of seeing them as obstacles to be avoided, we see them as opportunities for growth and refinement. We understand that our present sufferings are nothing compared to the glory that awaits us in eternity.

One of the most profound aspects of living with eternity in view is the way it changes how we view death. Instead of fearing death, we see it as a doorway to eternal life with God. We have hope beyond the grave, knowing that death has been swallowed up in victory through the resurrection of Jesus Christ.

So how do we live with eternity in view? It starts with a daily surrender to God, acknowledging His lordship over our lives. It involves seeking His Kingdom above all else and trusting Him to provide for our needs. It means living with a sense of urgency, knowing that our time on this earth is short, and that we must make the most of every opportunity to share the love of Christ with others.

Living with eternity in view is a radical way to live, but it's also a deeply fulfilling and meaningful way to live. It's about living for something greater than ourselves, something that transcends this life and extends into eternity. May we all strive to live with eternity in view, seeking to glorify God in all that we do and to store up treasure in heaven where it will last for eternity. May we be the fragrance of Christ in all that we say and do.

# Gratitude for Scars

In the intricate design of our lives, we often find ourselves chasing after moments of light—victories, joyous occasions, and experiences that uplift our spirits. Yet, intertwined with these moments are the shadows—the losses, the heartaches, the wounds that leave their mark on our souls. These scars, akin to the stars in a constellation, can sometimes feel like reminders of our imperfections and vulnerabilities.

But what if, instead of seeing them as flaws, we viewed our scars as integral to our story? What if they were the marks that bear witness to our journey, our trials, and our triumphs? Consider the story of Christ, who bore scars in his hands and side, marks of His sacrifice and victory over death. These scars, far from diminishing His glory, are symbols of His love and redemption for us.

Our scars, too, can be seen in this light. Each one speaks of a battle fought, a lesson learned, and a faith deepened. They are signs of our resilience, reminders that through Christ, we can overcome any adversity. When we view our scars through the lens of faith, they become symbols of our transformation, and testaments to God's grace working in us.

Acknowledging our scars does not erase the pain of the past. Scars are reminders of the wounds we have endured. But in Christ, we find healing and redemption. Our scars become reminders of His love and His power to transform our brokenness into something beautiful.

THE TAPESTRY OF LIFE

So, the next time you look upon your scars, remember the scars of Christ. Remember that through His wounds, we are healed. Let your scars be a source of thanksgiving, a reminder of God's faithfulness, and a repository of hope for yourself and others

# The Gift of Time

Time is a mysterious and profound gift. It flows like a river, carrying us along its currents, shaping our experiences, and molding our lives. Yet, despite its seemingly constant presence, time is elusive and intangible, slipping through our fingers like grains of sand.

In our fast-paced world, it is easy to view time as a commodity to be spent wisely or squandered thoughtlessly. We rush from one task to the next, always chasing the next deadline, the next goal, and the next achievement. But in our relentless pursuit of productivity, we often overlook the true essence of time.

Time is not merely a measure of moments passed or moments yet to come. It is a precious gift, a sacred space in which we are invited to dwell fully and deeply. Each moment is pregnant with possibility, offering us the chance to embrace life in all its richness and complexity.

In the Bible, Ecclesiastes tells us, "There is a time for everything, and a season for every activity under the heavens." This wisdom reminds us that time is not linear but cyclical, moving in rhythms and patterns that reflect the natural order of the universe.

As we navigate the passage of time, we are called to be mindful of its fleeting nature. The psalmist writes, "Teach us to number our days, that we may gain a heart of wisdom." This is an invitation to live each day with intention and purpose, recognizing that our time on earth is limited and precious.

But time is not just a finite resource to be managed; it is also a source of grace and blessing. In the book of Isaiah, God declares, "I

# The Tapestry of Life

am the Lord your God, who teaches you what is best for you, who directs you in the way you should go." This is a reminder that God is present in every moment of our lives, guiding us, sustaining us, and showering us with love.

When we view time through the lens of faith, we see that each moment is infused with divine significance. Every sunrise is a testament to God's faithfulness, every sunset a reminder of His grace. In the hustle and bustle of daily life, it is easy to lose sight of these truths. But when we pause and reflect on the nature of time, we begin to see that every moment is a gift, every second a chance to experience the wonder of God's creation.

So let us embrace the gift of time with open hearts and minds, cherishing each moment as a precious jewel. Let us not be consumed by busyness or distracted by trivialities, but instead, let us live each day with gratitude and awe, knowing that we are held in the loving embrace of the One who created time itself.

May we be mindful of the passage of time, grateful for its blessings, and faithful in our stewardship of its fleeting moments. And may we always remember that time is not our enemy but our friend, leading us ever closer to the eternal embrace of our Creator.

# The Challenge of Belief

In the journey of faith, we often find ourselves grappling with the challenge of belief. Why is believing so difficult? Why does being a person who has made the choice to worship a personal, Biblical God feel like such a troublesome task at times? We are often confronted with the harsh realities of life—adversity, suffering, and pain. How does difficulty impact the already daunting task of believing? How do we maintain our faith in the face of adversity?

For people who endure hardship and suffering, there is no guarantee that they will emerge from difficulty with their faith intact. Adversity has a way of shaking the foundations of our faith. When we are faced with challenges that seem insurmountable, when our prayers seem to go unanswered, and when we see suffering and injustice in the world, it can be tempting to question the very existence of a loving and benevolent God. We may wonder why a loving God would allow such pain and suffering to exist, why prayers seem to go unanswered, and why bad things happen to good people.

In the midst of adversity, the challenge of belief is magnified. The doubts and questions that we may have wrestled with in times of ease are brought into sharp focus. We are forced to confront the limitations of our understanding, to grapple with the seeming silence of Heaven. So often, belief can feel like a fragile thing, easily shattered by the harsh realities of life.

Believing—already a difficult challenge for some people even in the best of times—asks us to trust in an unseen God, to surrender our will to a greater purpose. For many of us, this is the ultimate

# The Tapestry of Life

challenge—to let go of our need for certainty and control, and instead embrace a posture of humility and trust.

And yet, it is in the crucible of adversity that our faith is truly tested and refined. It is easy to believe when life is going well, when our prayers are answered, and when everything is going according to plan. But true faith is forged in the fires of adversity, when everything that we hold dear is threatened, and when our faith is stretched to its breaking point.

So, how do we maintain our faith in the face of adversity? How do we find belief in the midst of suffering? The answer lies in embracing the mystery of faith, in acknowledging that there are truths that lie beyond our comprehension. It lies in finding meaning and purpose in the midst of suffering, in recognizing that our pain is not meaningless, but rather a part of a larger, redemptive story.

It also lies in finding community and support in our faith journey. In times of adversity, we can draw strength from those around us, from the stories of others who have walked similar paths, and from the knowledge that we are not alone in our struggles. We can find comfort in the belief that there is a greater purpose at work in the world, even when we cannot see it or understand it.

The challenge of belief in the face of adversity is perhaps one of the greatest tests we will ever face. It is a test that demands everything of us—our intellect, our emotions, and our will. It is a test that requires us to confront our deepest fears and doubts, to grapple with the mysteries of faith, and to find meaning and purpose in the midst of suffering.

And yet, it is also a test that offers the greatest rewards. For in facing the challenge of belief in adversity, we are drawn into a deeper relationship with God. We are invited to see the world through eyes of faith, to trust in a higher purpose that transcends our understanding. We are challenged to find beauty in the midst of pain, hope in the midst of despair, and love in the midst of suffering.

So let us embrace the challenge of belief in adversity, knowing that in doing so, we are not alone. We are surrounded by a cloud of witnesses who have gone before us, who have faced similar challenges and emerged with their faith intact. And we are held in the loving embrace of a God who walks with us through the darkest valleys and leads us into the light.

May we find the courage to believe in the face of doubt, the strength to hope in the face of despair, and the faith to love in the face of suffering. And may we emerge from the apprenticeship of adversity with our faith stronger, our hope brighter, and our love deeper than ever before.

# God's Comfort for Weary Souls

In the quiet moments of our lives, when the noise of the world fades away, and our hearts are laid bare, we often find that our spirits are weary from the journey. We carry with us the weight of our past, the burdens of our present, and the uncertainties of our future. We are like travelers on a long and arduous journey, longing for rest and renewal.

It's the weariness of a heart that has loved and lost, that has been broken and bruised by the trials of life. It's the weariness of a mind that is constantly racing, trying to make sense of a world that often seems senseless.

It's the weariness of a caregiver tending to an elderly parent, heart heavy with the weight of responsibility, yet full of love and compassion. It's the weariness of a soul that has seen too much suffering, too much pain, and too much injustice in the world. It's the weariness of a heart that has been broken and bruised, yet still beats with hope and resilience.

It's the weariness of a spirit that is adrift, searching for meaning and purpose in a world that can be cruel and unforgiving. It's the weariness of a soul that longs for peace, for rest, and for a moment of respite from the storms that rage both within and without. It's the weariness of a traveler who has journeyed long and hard, feet blistered and legs aching, longing for a place to rest.

But in the midst of our weariness, there is hope. For we are not alone on this journey. We are accompanied by a God who walks beside us, offering us rest and renewal. In the words of the psalmist, "He makes me lie down in green pastures, he leads me beside quiet waters, he refreshes my soul" (Psalm 23:2-3). God's grace is a balm for our weary souls. It is a gentle reminder that we are loved, valued, and cherished. It is a source of strength and comfort, a beacon of hope in the darkest of nights. It is a promise that, no matter how weary we may be, we are never beyond the reach of God's grace.

So let us rest in that grace. Let us lay down our burdens and surrender our weariness to the God who cares for us. Let us find renewal in the quiet moments of prayer and reflection, knowing that we are held in the loving embrace of our Creator.

May our weary souls find rest in the grace of God, and may we be renewed and refreshed for the journey ahead.

# Navigating Disappointment with Grace

Disappointment is a universal human experience, a guest that arrives uninvited, often leaving a lingering mark on our hearts. It can be a profound teacher, offering us a choice: to resist its presence or to embrace its lessons. How we navigate disappointment can shape our character and deepen our understanding of grace.

When disappointment knocks on our door, it brings a range of emotions. There's the initial shock, a feeling of disbelief that things didn't turn out as hoped. This can quickly give way to sadness, a heaviness in the heart that weighs us down. We may feel anger, directed at ourselves, others, or even at the circumstances beyond our control. These emotions are natural, part of the human experience, but they need not define our response.

In the depths of disappointment, there is an opportunity for growth. It is at this juncture that we can choose to lean into grace, to embrace the discomfort as a pathway to deeper understanding of the tapestry of life woven by the Master. It is a chance to acknowledge our vulnerability, to recognize that we are not in control of everything, and that is okay.

Grace meets us in our disappointment, offering us a hand to hold as we navigate the stormy seas of unmet expectations. It reminds us that we are not alone in our struggles, that others have walked this path before us. Grace whispers words of comfort, gently reminding us that this too shall pass, and that there is beauty In the brokenness.

Handling disappointment with grace does not mean denying our emotions or pretending that everything is fine. It means allowing ourselves to feel deeply, to acknowledge the pain, but not to be consumed by it. It means finding strength in our vulnerability, in the recognition that we are human, imperfect, and in need of grace . . . in need of God and His help. In the embrace of grace, we find the courage to forgive—ourselves, others, and even the situation. Forgiveness does not mean forgetting or condoning what has happened; rather, it is a choice to release the burden of anger and resentment that weighs us down. It is a choice to free ourselves from the chains of the past, to make room for new beginnings.

As we journey through life, disappointment will inevitably cross our path. It is how we choose to respond that defines us. Will we allow disappointment to harden our hearts, or will we embrace it as a teacher, guiding us toward greater understanding and compassion? The choice is ours, but the path of grace is always open, ready to lead us home.

# Waiting in the Midst of the Storm

In life, we often find ourselves in the midst of storms—metaphorical tempests of uncertainty, fear, and doubt. These storms can take many forms: a health crisis, a period of financial hardship, the loss of a loved one, or simply a season of profound change. It can feel like the storm will never end, that the dark clouds will block out the sun forever.

Yet, just as in nature, no storm lasts forever. There comes a moment when the wind begins to calm, the rain starts to ease, and the clouds slowly part to reveal the light of the sun once more. It is in the tranquility of such moments that we are reminded of the beauty of waiting for the storm to pass.

Waiting for the storm teaches us patience, the value of endurance, and the importance of faith. It reminds us that, even in our darkest moments, there is light on the horizon. It teaches us to trust that, just as the storm eventually gives way to clear skies, so too will our troubles eventually fade away.

But waiting for the storm is not simply about enduring hardship. It is also about finding peace in the midst of chaos. It is about learning to be still, to quiet our minds and hearts, and to listen for the voice of calm that speaks to us even in the midst of the storm.

In the Bible, Jesus demonstrates this kind of peace when He calms the stormy sea. In the midst of a raging tempest, He sleeps peacefully in the boat, untroubled by the chaos around Him. When

His disciples wake Him in fear, He simply speaks to the storm, "Peace, be still," and the winds and waves obey Him. This story reminds us that even in the most turbulent times, we can find peace in our relationship with God. We can trust that God is with us in the storm, guiding us, protecting us, and leading us to calmer waters.

So, as we wait for the storm to pass, let us hold fast to the hope that sustains us. Let us trust in the promise of brighter days ahead. And let us find peace in the knowledge that, no matter how fierce the storm may be, it is only temporary. The sun will shine again, and we will emerge from the darkness stronger, wiser, and more grateful for the light.

# THE TRANSFORMATIVE LOVE OF GOD

Being greatly loved by God is a transformative realization that reshapes how we see ourselves, others, and the world around us. This profound truth, woven throughout Scripture, can be a source of immense comfort and strength, especially in times of trial and uncertainty. God's love is not just a theological concept but a living, vibrant reality that embraces us with warmth and tenderness, especially in our most vulnerable moments.

The Bible often speaks of God's love in terms of depth and intensity. In Ephesians 3:17–19, Paul prays that believers "may have power, together with all the Lord's holy people, to grasp how wide and long and high and deep is the love of Christ, and to know this love that surpasses knowledge—that you may be filled to the measure of all the fullness of God." The dimensions of God's love are beyond comprehension, yet they invite us to explore and experience it daily. God's love is not a passive, distant affection but an active, pursuing love—immeasurable, inexhaustible, and always reaching out to us, no matter where we are or what we have done.

Consider the parable of the lost sheep in Luke 15:3–7. The shepherd leaves the ninety-nine to find the one lost sheep, illustrating God's relentless pursuit of us. This story isn't just about sheep; it's about us. Each of us is the one sheep, so precious to God that He would traverse any distance to bring us back. This is a love that sees us, knows us by name, and never gives up on us. This narrative underscores that we are not just loved in a general sense but are individually known and cherished. Each of us matters to God, and He seeks us out when we stray.

This love is also demonstrated supremely in the life, death, and resurrection of Jesus Christ. In Romans 5:8, we read, "But God demonstrates his own love for us in this: While we were still sinners, Christ died for us." This verse encapsulates the self-sacrificial nature of God's love. Even when we were at our worst, God gave His best. Jesus' sacrifice on the cross is the ultimate expression of God's love, breaking the power of sin and death, and opening the way for us to have a restored relationship with Him.

Understanding we are greatly loved by God affects our identity. We are not defined by our failures or successes, our past mistakes, or even our present circumstances. Instead, our identity is rooted in being beloved children of God. 1 John 3:1 says, "See what great love the Father has lavished on us, that we should be called children of God! And that is what we are!" This status is not something we earn but something we receive by grace. Knowing we are greatly loved by God transforms our identity. Our destiny is determined as children of the living God—not by fears, nor missteps, or the labels the world places on us.

Living in the awareness of God's great love transforms our interactions with others. We are called to love because we have been loved. In John 13:34–35, Jesus commands, "A new command I give you: Love one another. As I have loved you, so you must love one another. By this everyone will know that you are my disciples if you love one another." Our love for others becomes a testimony of God's love at work within us. It propels us to acts of kindness, forgiveness, and compassion, reflecting the heart of God to a hurting world.

Moreover, being greatly loved by God provides security and hope. Romans 8:38–39 reassures us, "For I am convinced that neither death nor life, neither angels nor demons, neither the present nor the future, nor any powers, neither height nor depth, nor anything else in all creation, will be able to separate us from the love of God that is in Christ Jesus our Lord." No matter what we face, we can rest in the assurance that God's love for us is unchanging and undefeatable.

To be greatly loved by God is to be enveloped in a love that is vast, active, sacrificial, identity-shaping, and transformative. It is a love that calls us to love others and grants us unwavering security.

Feel the weight of those words. We are children of God, cherished and valued beyond measure, not because of anything we have done but because of who He is. May we daily bask in this truth, letting it permeate every aspect of our lives.

# Divine Interruptions

In our busy lives, interruptions are often seen as unwelcome intrusions, disrupting our carefully planned schedules and routines. We tend to view them as obstacles to our goals, hindrances to our progress. However, what if we were to shift our perspective and see these interruptions as divine interventions?

The concept of divine interruptions challenges us to see beyond the surface-level inconvenience and recognize that these disruptions might be opportunities in disguise. They could be moments when God is trying to get our attention, redirect our path, or teach us valuable lessons.

Think back to moments in your life when things didn't go as planned. Perhaps you missed a flight, got stuck in traffic, or had to deal with an unexpected setback at work. In those moments, it's easy to feel frustrated and defeated. But what if those interruptions were God's way of protecting you from harm, leading you to a better opportunity, or teaching you patience and resilience?

The story of Joseph in the Bible is a powerful example of how divine interruptions can lead to unexpected blessings. Joseph's story begins with him being sold into slavery by his jealous brothers. This interruption in Joseph's life could have been seen as a tragedy, but Joseph remained faithful to God and trusted that His plan was at work.

Despite facing many hardships, including being wrongly imprisoned, Joseph continued to trust in God's plan for his life. In the end, Joseph's faithfulness was rewarded, and he was elevated to a position of great authority in Egypt, where he was able to save his family and many others from famine.

Joseph's story reminds us that divine interruptions are often God's way of guiding us toward His greater purpose. These interruptions may not make sense to us in the moment, but if we remain faithful and trust in God's plan, we can be confident that He is leading us toward something greater than we could ever imagine.

As we face interruptions in our own lives, let us remember Joseph's example and trust that God is at work, even in the midst of chaos and uncertainty. Let us trust that God's plans for us are good, even when they seem to diverge from our own. May we learn to see these interruptions as divine appointments, moments when God is present, and at work in our lives in ways we may not immediately understand.

Let us pray: Dear God, help us to recognize Your hand in the interruptions of our lives. Give us the wisdom to see beyond the immediate inconvenience and understand Your greater purpose for us. Help us to trust in Your goodness and embrace these interruptions as opportunities for growth and blessing.

Amen.

# The Whirlwind of the Unknown

Life is full of surprises—some joyful, others challenging. We make plans, set goals, and envision our futures, but often, the unexpected comes knocking at our door. It could be a sudden change in circumstances, an unexpected health problem, an unforeseen obstacle, or a complete detour from the path we had envisioned.

The unexpected has a way of unsettling us, stirring up a whirlwind of emotions. It can leave us feeling anxious, overwhelmed, and unsure of what the future holds. The unknown path ahead can seem daunting, filled with uncertainty and fear.

In these moments, it's important to remember that we are not alone. God is with us, walking beside us through the unknown. He sees our fears, our doubts, and our struggles, and He offers us His peace, a peace that surpasses all understanding.

Finding peace in the unknown begins with trust—trust in God's goodness, trust in His wisdom, and trust in His plan for our lives. It means letting go of our need for control and surrendering to His will, even when we don't understand it.

The emotional toll of the unknown can be heavy, but God invites us to cast our burdens upon Him, for He cares for us. He understands our fears and our struggles, and He offers us His comfort and His strength to carry us through. So, as you navigate the unknown path ahead, lean into God's embrace. Trust in His unfailing love and His promise to guide you. Find peace in knowing that He is working all things together for your good, even when you can't see it.

Prayer:

Heavenly Father, help us to trust in Your plan for our lives, even when the unexpected happens. Give us the faith to embrace the unknown, knowing that You are with us every step of the way. Help us to surrender our plans to Your will, trusting that Your ways are higher than our ways. Amen.

# Spiritual Fingerprints

In the vast tapestry of existence, each of us is a unique thread, weaving our way through time and space, leaving behind a trail of experiences and interactions that shape the world around us. Just as no two physical fingerprints are alike, so too are our spiritual fingerprints—the imprint of our soul on the fabric of the universe.

Our spiritual fingerprints are the essence of who we are, the sum total of our thoughts, words, and actions. They are the marks we leave on the lives of others, the legacy we create, and the impact we have on the world. Just as a fingerprint can be used to identify a person, our spiritual fingerprints reveal the essence of our being, the core of our identity.

Each day, we have the opportunity to leave a positive imprint on the world through our actions. A kind word, a helping hand, or a compassionate gesture—these are the marks of a life well-lived, the signs of a soul in tune with its true nature. When we act from a place of love and compassion, we leave behind a trail of God's light that illuminates the path for others to follow.

But our spiritual fingerprints are not just about the impact we have on the world; they are also about the impact the world has on us. Every experience we have, every person we meet, leaves a mark on our soul, shaping us into the person we are meant to be. Just as a fingerprint is a record of a person's unique identity, our spiritual fingerprints are a record of our unique journey through life.

It is important to remember that our spiritual fingerprints are not fixed; they are constantly evolving and changing as we grow and learn. What we leave behind today may not be the same as what we leave behind tomorrow. This is a reminder that we are always a work in progress, always striving to become the best version of ourselves.

Each day, we have the opportunity to reflect God's love and grace to the world through our actions. When we act with kindness, compassion, and generosity, we are reflecting God's image in which we are created. Just as a fingerprint is a unique identifier, our actions are a unique expression of God's love working through us.

As we go about our days, let us be mindful of the imprint we are leaving on the world. Let us strive to leave behind a trail of love, compassion, and grace, knowing that we are reflections of God's love in the world, and that our spiritual fingerprints will forever be a part of the tapestry of existence.

# Providing Sanctuary

In ancient times, a sanctuary was a sacred place, a holy refuge where individuals sought protection from harm. In our modern world, often marked by turmoil and uncertainty, the role of sanctuary has become increasingly vital. As individuals seeking emotionally safe spaces and refuge, we are also called to be the bearers of sanctuary, offering a haven for others amidst life's storms.

To provide sanctuary for others is to embody empathy, compassion, and understanding. It is to create a space where individuals feel accepted, valued, and safe. Just as we seek sanctuary in our own lives, we have the capacity to become sanctuaries for those around us.

Providing sanctuary for others requires us to cultivate a spirit of hospitality. It is about creating an environment where people feel welcomed, where they can be themselves without fear of judgment or rejection. It is about listening with an open heart, offering a shoulder to lean on, and being a source of light in times of darkness.

Sanctuary is not just about physical spaces; it is about the atmosphere we create with our words, our actions, and our presence. It is being fully present with others, offering them our undivided attention and genuine care.

One of the most powerful ways we can provide sanctuary for others is through the gift of presence. Simply being there for someone, offering a listening ear and a caring heart, can make a world of difference. In a world that often feels chaotic and overwhelming, the simple act of being present can be a profound source of comfort and reassurance.

Providing sanctuary for others also involves creating a sense of belonging. It is about fostering a community where everyone feels valued and respected, where diversity is celebrated, and where everyone has a place at the table. It is about building bridges of understanding and compassion, reaching out to those who are marginalized or forgotten, and standing up for justice and equality.

In ministering Christ, we become extensions of His sanctuary, offering warmth and kindness to those around us. We become the hands that offer help, the ears that listen without judgment, and the hearts that overflow with love. Through our actions, we create a sanctuary of acceptance and belonging, where everyone is welcomed with open arms.

Christ's ministry is a sanctuary of transformation, where brokenness is healed, and wounds are mended. It is a sanctuary of forgiveness, where mistakes are met with grace, and second chances are freely given. In ministering Christ, we invite others into this sanctuary of transformation, offering them the same love and compassion that Christ has shown us.

Ministering Christ provides sanctuary through His boundless love, compassion, and transformative power. His ministry offers refuge for the weary, healing for the broken, and hope for the hopeless. As we embody His love and compassion in our own lives, we become sanctuaries for others, offering warmth, acceptance, and the promise of a life renewed by His grace.

# A Lifetime of Friends

Friendships are not merely connections; they are the threads that weave a sacred tapestry of our lives. They bring color to our existence, depth to our experiences, and meaning to our journey. In the fabric of life, treasured friendships are the intricate patterns that make each day more beautiful, more profound.

Think of the friends who have graced your life, the ones who have walked with you through the seasons, sharing laughter under the sun, and finding comfort in each other's company under the stars. These friends are more than companions; they are the mirrors that reflect our true selves, the anchors that keep us grounded, and the sails that help us navigate the seas of life.

In Ecclesiastes 4:9-10, we are reminded of the profound impact of companionship. Just as two are better than one, so too are friends better together, offering each other strength, support, and unwavering love. They are the ones who lift us up when we fall, who celebrate our victories as if they were their own, and who remind us that we are never alone.

Treasured friendships are a testament to the beauty of human connection, the power of shared experiences, and the gift of unconditional love. They remind us that we are seen, known, and deeply loved for who we are, flaws and all. They teach us empathy, compassion, and the true meaning of friendship.

Today, take a moment to reflect on the treasured friendships in your life. Give thanks for the friends who have shaped you, supported you, and loved you unconditionally. And may you, in turn,

# The Tapestry of Life

be a friend who offers the same kind of love and support to those around you.

In treasured friendships, we find a glimpse of God's love that binds us all together. Let us cherish these friendships, nurturing them with care, gratitude, and deep appreciation for the blessings they bring to our lives.

# Navigating the Storms of Life

Scripture: "For God is not a God of confusion but of peace." — 1 Corinthians 14:33

In the throes of a storm, both literal and metaphorical, confusion can reign supreme. We are bombarded with conflicting information, unsure of which path to take or whom to trust. The recent confusion regarding weather sources—what weather sources to trust in the midst of a storm—is just one example of how disconcerting it can be when clarity eludes us.

Confusion is disorienting. It is like a turbulent sea, tossing us to and fro with its conflicting currents. It can be disorienting, leaving us unsure of which way to turn. It clouds our judgment and obscures the way forward. It can be especially unsettling when the stakes are high, such as during severe weather when our safety is on the line. In such moments, we often turn to external sources for guidance, whether it be weather apps, TV stations, or websites. However, as we've experienced, even these sources can sometimes lead to further confusion.

In times of confusion, it's essential to remember that God is a God of peace, not confusion. While the storms of life may rage around us, God offers us a sense of calm amidst the chaos. Just as a lighthouse guides ships safely to shore in a storm, so too can God's presence guide us through the tumult of confusion.

Turning to our faith in God can help us navigate the storms of confusion. Through prayer and reflection, we can find the clarity we seek. It may not always provide immediate answers, but it can offer us a sense of peace and assurance that God is with us, guiding us through the storm.

In times of confusion, it can be tempting to rely solely on our own understanding or the guidance of others. However, true peace comes from trusting in God's guidance. By turning to our faith and seeking God's presence, we can find the clarity and peace we seek, even in the midst of life's storms.

# Liminal Spaces

Have you ever noticed how certain moments or places in life feel like you're standing on the threshold of something new and unknown? They can be unsettling, like the pause between heartbeats, yet they are also profoundly sacred, offering us a unique opportunity to encounter God in a deeper way.

In the tapestry of life, there are moments and places that exist in-between, where the familiar fades into the unknown, and God's presence feels palpable. These are liminal spaces, thresholds of transformation, where we stand on the cusp of change, growth, and deeper spiritual understanding. They are those in-between times when the old has passed away, and the new has not yet fully arrived.

The Bible is replete with stories of liminality. The Israelites stood at the edge of the Red Sea, the wilderness stretching before them—a liminal space of uncertainty and faith. Mary, pregnant with Jesus, journeyed to Bethlehem, embodying the liminal space between the old and the new, the promise and fulfillment. Even Jesus Himself spent forty days in the wilderness, a liminal time of testing and preparation, before beginning His ministry.

Liminal spaces are part of our journey of faith too. They can be seasons of waiting, times of uncertainty, or moments of decision. They challenge us to let go of our need for control and to trust in God's timing and provision. They remind us that faith is not about having all the answers but about trusting in the One who does.

Liminal spaces are not comfortable; they challenge us to let go of the familiar and step into the unknown. They invite us to trust in God's guidance, even when the path ahead is shrouded in uncertainty. It is in these moments of transition that our faith is refined, our trust deepened, and our hearts opened to the movement of the Spirit.

But liminal spaces are also sacred; they are thin places where the veil between heaven and earth seems to lift. They are moments of divine encounter, where God meets us in our vulnerability and whispers words of comfort and assurance. It is in these in-between places that we are reminded of God's faithfulness, His presence with us in every season of life.

As Christians, we are called to embrace liminal spaces—to see them not as obstacles to be overcome but as opportunities for growth and transformation. Like the caterpillar in the chrysalis, we are being transformed into something new, something beautiful, by the renewing work of the Holy Spirit.

So, as you find yourself in a liminal space today, whether it be a season of waiting, a moment of transition, or a place of uncertainty, embrace it. Trust that God is with you in the midst of it, guiding you, shaping you, and preparing you for what lies ahead. And remember, the God who led His people through the wilderness, who was born in a stable, who conquered death itself, is with you in your liminal space, leading you from glory to glory.

# IN THE SHADOW OF BETRAYAL

Betrayal is a cavernous abyss that swallows us whole, leaving us lost in the darkness of shattered trust and fractured relationships. Judas' betrayal of Jesus is a chilling reminder of the depths to which human treachery can sink. Judas, a disciple who walked side by side with Jesus, shared meals with Him, and witnessed His miracles, chose to betray Him with a kiss—a symbol of intimacy twisted into an instrument of betrayal.

The wounds of betrayal are deep because they come from someone we least expect. Judas was part of Jesus' inner circle, sharing meals, witnessing miracles, and hearing His teachings. Yet, in a moment of weakness, he betrayed his friend, his teacher, and his Lord.

The wounds of betrayal are not mere scratches on the surface of our souls; they are deep gashes that bleed into every aspect of our being. They leave us gasping for breath, grappling with questions that have no easy answers. "How could they do this to me?", "Was our bond nothing but a façade?", and "Can I ever trust again?"

In the shadow of betrayal, we find Jesus, who knows the agony of betrayal firsthand. He was betrayed by one of His closest companions, yet He responded, not with bitterness or vengeance, but with love and forgiveness. He did not allow Judas' betrayal to derail His mission of redemption.

Our Lord invites us to bring our wounds of betrayal to Him. He understands our pain and offers healing. He can turn our scars into stories of grace and redemption. He can teach us to forgive as He forgave, to love as He loved.

As we traverse the path of this day, let us journey through the abyss of betrayal with Jesus by our side. Let us confront the darkness within us and around us, knowing that His light shines brightest in the darkest of nights. Let us find comfort in His embrace, knowing that His love is greater than any betrayal we may endure. In the crucible of betrayal, may we find the courage to forgive, the strength to love, and the grace to heal.

# Fellow Pilgrims in the Journey of Life

In our earthly pilgrimage, we are blessed with companions who walk alongside us, sharing the joys and sorrows of our journey. These are the people whose presence enriches our lives, whose kindness and love illuminate our path. Some have been a constant presence for decades.

Think of those who have stood by you in moments of trial, offering a comforting hand, and a listening ear. They are the ones who remind us that we are not alone, that there is strength in unity, and solace in shared burdens.

Our companions come in various forms—family, friends, mentors, and even strangers whose paths intersect with ours for a brief but meaningful moment. Each one plays a unique role in shaping our experiences and helping us grow.

They teach us about love and compassion, showing us how to care for others selflessly. They inspire us to be better, to strive for greatness, and to never lose hope, no matter how challenging the road may seem.

In their presence, we find acceptance and understanding, a safe harbor where we can be ourselves without fear of judgment. They see us for who we truly are, embracing our flaws and imperfections, and loving us all the more for them.

Through their words and actions, our companions reveal the beauty of human connection, reminding us of our inherent need for community and fellowship. They remind us that we are all interconnected, that our lives are intertwined in a tapestry of shared experiences and shared humanity.

As we journey through life, let us cherish the companions who grace our path, for they are a treasured gift from God. Let us be grateful for their presence, for the light they bring into our lives, and the love they bestow upon us.

May we also strive to be good companions to others, offering our love and support unconditionally. Let us be a beacon of hope and kindness, a source of strength and comfort to those in need.

And when our earthly journey comes to an end, may we look back on our lives with gratitude for the companions who walked with us, knowing that we were never truly alone, but always surrounded by the love of our fellow travelers.

# The Nearness of God

Our hearts are sacred spaces, holding our deepest longings, fears, and joys. In moments of solitude, we often turn inward, seeking to understand ourselves better. Yet, even in our most intimate moments with ourselves, God is there, intimately acquainted with all our ways. The psalmist beautifully captures this truth, declaring, "You discern my going out and my lying down; you are familiar with all my ways" (Psalm 139:3). God's closeness is not dependent on our awareness or acknowledgment but is a constant reality. He knows us better than we know ourselves. He understands our thoughts from afar and is intimately acquainted with all our ways (Psalm 139:2-3). This profound truth should transform how we perceive and experience our lives.

Imagine a love that knows no bounds, a presence that is always with you, or a friend who understands you completely. This is the reality of God's closeness. He is not a distant deity but a loving Father who is deeply invested in every aspect of our lives. In our moments of solitude, when we wrestle with our thoughts and emotions, God is there, offering comfort and peace. In our moments of joy, when our hearts overflow with gratitude, God is there, rejoicing with us. In our moments of fear, when we feel overwhelmed by life's uncertainties, God is there, offering strength and courage.

Knowing that God is closer to us than our own hearts should fill us with awe and gratitude. It should remind us that we are never alone, never forgotten. God's love is constant, unwavering, and unconditional.

As you go about your day, take comfort in the nearness of God. Remember that He is with you always, guiding you, comforting you, and loving you more deeply than you can imagine. Let this truth transform how you perceive and experience your life, knowing that you are always held in the palm of God's hand.

# The Sacred Dance of Everyday Existence

In the tapestry of our daily lives, there exists a sacred dance that unfolds with each passing moment. This dance is not flashy or grand; it is quiet, subtle, and often overlooked. It is the dance of everyday existence, where the mundane and the sacred intertwine in a beautiful choreography of life.

God is not separate from our daily lives; God is present in every moment, in every action. When we take the time to notice the beauty around us, we are witnessing the handiwork of the Divine. When we feel a sense of peace and contentment, we are experiencing the presence of God within us.

Imagine the simple act of washing dishes. At first glance, it may seem like a menial task, devoid of any significance. But if we approach it with mindfulness and presence, we can see that it is a dance of cleansing and renewal, a reminder of the importance of tending to the everyday aspects of our lives with care and attention.

In the sacred dance of everyday existence, God is the choreographer, guiding our steps and leading us towards a deeper understanding of ourselves and the world around us. God is the music that fills our hearts with joy and our souls with peace, reminding us that we are never alone, that we are always loved.

As we move through our day, let us be mindful of this sacred dance that surrounds us. In the laughter of a friend, we hear the music of connection and community. In the beauty of a sunset, we see the artistry of creation. In the silence of a moment alone, we feel the presence of God.

When we learn to see the sacred dance of everyday existence, we open ourselves up to a deeper experience of life. We begin to see that every moment is infused with meaning and purpose, and that even the most ordinary of tasks can be a source of profound beauty and grace.

When we embrace the presence of God in our lives, we begin to see the world in a new light. We see that every moment is an opportunity for connection, for growth, and for transformation. We see that even in the midst of hardship and struggle, there is a divine purpose at work, guiding us towards a greater understanding of ourselves and our place in the world.

May we always remember that God is with us, in every moment, in every breath. May we embrace the sacred dance of everyday existence, and may we find joy and fulfillment in the simple moments that make up our lives.

Amen.

# When Life Doesn't Make Sense

There are moments in life when no matter how hard we try, things just don't seem to make sense. It's like trying to solve a puzzle with missing pieces—frustrating, confusing, and disheartening. We pour our hearts into our work, our relationships, our dreams, only to be met with obstacles and setbacks that leave us feeling defeated and lost.

I've been there, in the throes of despair when it feels like the world is crashing down around me. I've questioned my worth, my abilities, and my purpose, wondering why my best efforts never seem to be enough. It's in those sleepless nights that I've felt the weight of disappointment pressing down on me, making it hard to breathe, and hard to see a way forward.

The feelings of inadequacy and self-doubt cut deep, like a jagged knife slicing through the fabric of my being. They whisper cruel lies, telling me I am not enough, that I will never be enough. They plant seeds of doubt in my mind, making me question every decision, every action, and every thought.

The fear of failure becomes a constant companion, its shadow looming large over every decision made and every action taken. It's a paralyzing fear; one that threatens to derail dreams and living life to the fullest. My worth feels like a fragile thing, easily shattered by the slightest breeze. I wonder if I have what it takes to navigate the challenges of life, if I have the strength to face the trials that lie ahead.

I've also experienced the light of God's presence shining through. I've felt His comforting embrace, reminding me that I am not alone, and that He is with me, guiding me, and strengthening me. I've learned to trust in His plan, even when it doesn't make sense to me.

The story of Joseph in the Bible has been a source of comfort and inspiration to me in those dark periods. Joseph endured years of hardship and betrayal, sold into slavery by his own brothers and unjustly imprisoned. Yet, through it all, Joseph remained faithful to God, trusting in His plan. And in the end, God used Joseph's suffering to save his family and fulfill His promise to him.

So, when life doesn't make sense, when you find yourself struggling to understand why things are happening the way they are, take heart. You are not alone. God is with you, walking beside you, and carrying you through the storm. Trust in Him, lean on Him, and let His love fill you with hope and strength for the journey ahead.

# Threads of Frailty and Fragility

In the tapestry of human existence, the threads of frailty and fragility are intricately woven. We are born into a world where disease, debilitation, pain, and suffering are not strangers but companions on our journey. We see loved ones struck down by illness, bodies weakened by age, and minds clouded by despair. They waste away until death takes them from us.

It is a journey marked by unexpected twists and turns, where the strongest among us can be brought to their knees by illness or injury, and where the brightest lights can be dimmed by the shadows of despair. When our bodies betray us and our spirits falter, we are often left wondering, "Where is God in all of this?"

It is in the wilderness of questioning and doubt that the light of grace shines most brightly. Grace is not the absence of suffering but the presence of God in the midst of it. It is the gentle whisper that says, "You are not alone. I am with you." It is the strength that upholds us when our own strength fails.

God does not promise us a life free from suffering, but He does promise to be with us in our suffering. He is the one Who weeps with us when we mourn, Who comforts us when we are in pain, and Who sustains us when we are weak.

Grace does not always take away our frailty and fragility, but it gives us the courage to face them. It is God's hand that reaches out to lift us up when we fall, His voice that speaks words of hope

# The Tapestry of Life

when all seems lost, and the Presence Who stands behind us when cannot see Him.

As we navigate the challenges of human life, may we remember that our frailty and fragility are not signs of God's absence but reminders of His presence. May we find comfort in the knowledge that we are held in the embrace of His grace, now and always.

(A personal note: There are several people who read these devotionals who are hurting badly, deeply from physical and emotional pain…experienced both in the past and in the present day. They have shared their personal stories of grave suffering, emotional scars, debilitation, devastating betrayal and abandonment, and the pain of watching loved ones fighting their last war with pain and suffering as they die.

You are in good company with people who question where God is when facing withering adversity. The books of Psalms and Lamentations speak often about God seeming far away, where we feel heaven's deafening silence.

In those books, as well as in Job, the answer to those heartfelt questions rests in the Person of God. A cold, theological answer concerning the problem of evil and badness in the world offers no solace, no comfort. We find rest for our souls in our relationship with God. In His very Person. It is here that we bring our questions, our pleas, and our pain.

In the midst of trials, calamities, suffering, heartache, pain, and betrayal…hold on to the Lord tightly, with all your being, and don't let go. Know that He has always been holding you…even when He seems far away. Ask Him for grace, encouragement, and hope.

This is my prayer for you. May God reveal Himself in a special way as you traverse the desolation of suffering. (Please know that I love you…that I pray for you…that I carry you with me in my heart.)

# WHEN THE WHEELS COME OFF

Life can often feel like a smooth ride down a familiar road. We grow accustomed to the rhythm of our routines, the comfort of the known. But then, without warning, the wheels come off. A sudden crisis, a devastating loss, a debilitating illness, or an unexpected turn of events shatters our sense of normalcy. In such circumstances, sometimes in the throes of crisis, we are faced with a choice: to despair or to seek grace.

It's natural to feel overwhelmed when life takes an unexpected turn. We may question why this is happening to us or feel angry at the unfairness of it all. But it is precisely in these moments of chaos and uncertainty that grace can shine brightest.

Grace is not a magical shield that protects us from pain and suffering. Instead, it is the inner strength that enables us to endure, to persevere, and to find meaning in the midst of adversity. When the wheels come off, grace invites us to look beyond our immediate circumstances and to see the bigger picture.

One of the most profound examples of grace, in the face of adversity, is found in the story of Viktor Frankl, a Holocaust survivor who found meaning and purpose in the midst of unimaginable suffering. Frankl wrote, "When we are no longer able to change a situation, we are challenged to change ourselves." (Frankl, Viktor E. *Man's Search for Meaning*. Boston: Beacon Press, 2006.) [KS11] In the darkest moments of his life, Frankl discovered a deep reservoir

# The Tapestry of Life

of grace that enabled him to find hope and meaning where others saw only despair.

Finding grace in times of crisis requires us to cultivate a spirit of resilience and gratitude. Instead of focusing on what we have lost, we can choose to be thankful for what remains. Instead of succumbing to bitterness and self-pity, we can choose to extend kindness and compassion to others.

As Christians, we understand grace as unmerited favor. Just as we receive grace freely from a loving God, so too are we called to extend grace to others, especially in their moments of need. When the wheels come off, grace invites us to be light in a world that can sometimes seem dark and hopeless.

Accepting grace when the wheels come off requires us to surrender our need for control and to trust in God's plan, even when we cannot see it. It means acknowledging our own limitations and weaknesses and allowing God's strength to work through us. It means finding peace in the midst of the storm, knowing that God is with us, guiding us, and sustaining us.

As we navigate the ups and downs of life, may we be reminded that grace is not a destination but a journey. It is not something we achieve but something we receive. And when the wheels come off, may we find comfort in the knowledge that we do not walk alone, but are held in the loving embrace of a grace that is infinite and eternal.

# Navigating the Beauty and Ugliness of Existence

Life is often likened to a tapestry, woven with threads of joy and sorrow, beauty and ugliness. While the beauty around us is often celebrated, the ugliness that creeps into our lives can be a source of struggle. This ugliness may manifest as pain, loss, suffering, failure, soured relationships, or even our own shortcomings. These periods of darkness can be deeply unsettling, shaking the very foundation of our beliefs and challenging our sense of purpose, leaving us feeling lost, disillusioned, and overwhelmed.

In these moments, we are confronted with the stark realities of human suffering, both personal and collective, forcing us to confront the fragility of our existence, the impermanence of our joys, and the harshness of our realities.

One of the most challenging aspects of dealing with life's ugliness is the feeling of powerlessness that often accompanies it. Faced with situations beyond our control, where the actions of others or the circumstances of life seem to conspire against us, it can be tempting to retreat into bitterness or resignation, closing ourselves off from the world in an attempt to protect ourselves from further harm.

Gratitude is one way to deal with life's ugliness. By focusing on the blessings that surround us, even in hardship, we can shift our perspective and find moments of beauty in unexpected places. Taking a moment each day to reflect on things we are grateful for, no matter how small, can soften life's harsh edges and bring a sense of peace and contentment.

Compassion is another powerful tool for navigating life's ugliness, both for ourselves and for others. When faced with difficult situations, it is easy to fall into self-criticism or judgment. However, practicing self-compassion allows us to treat ourselves with kindness and understanding, recognizing that we are all imperfect beings doing the best we can. Similarly, extending compassion to others helps us see beyond their outward actions or appearances, recognizing the humanity we all share.

In the face of life's ugliness, it can be easy to lose hope, believing that the darkness will never end. Yet, it is important to remember that even the darkest night is followed by the dawn. By holding onto hope and trusting in the resilience of the human spirit, bolstered by faith, we can find the strength to endure even the most difficult of times.

Dealing with life's ugliness is a deeply personal journey, and there is no one-size-fits-all solution. However, by embracing gratitude, practicing compassion, and holding onto hope, we can begin to transform ugliness into beauty, finding meaning and purpose in even the most challenging moments.

# When Hope Feels Like a Four-Letter Word

Hope is a powerful force, capable of guiding us through the darkest of times. Yet, for some, hope can feel like a four-letter word, a cruel illusion that only serves to disappoint. When life has been raw, unbelievably difficult, marred by suffering, and filled with disappointment and despair, it can be hard to hold on to hope, to believe that things will ever get better. But even in our darkest moments, hope is not lost.

For those who see hope as a four-letter word, it's important to remember that hope is not about wishful thinking or blind optimism. True hope is founded in faith, a deep-seated belief that God is present in our lives and working for our good. It is a hope that transcends our circumstances, grounded in the person of God, and a hope that sees beyond the darkness to the Light that lies ahead.

Like so many people in the Bible, we too can find hope in the midst of despair. We can take comfort in knowing that God is with us, even in our darkest moments, working for our good. We can find hope in the promises of Scripture, which assure us that God has a plan for our lives...a plan to prosper us and not to harm us, to give us hope and a future. In the throes of suffering, ask God to help you see a future despite the suffering, a future where you can experience grace while in the teeth of adversity. Your answers will be found in the person of God Himself.

When hope feels like a four-letter word, it can be helpful to turn to prayer. Prayer is a powerful means of grace, capable of lifting our spirits and renewing our hope. In prayer, we can pour out our hearts to God, expressing our fears, doubts, and frustrations. And in return, God offers us His peace, His comfort, and His hope.

The power of a loving, caring community cannot be overstated. It is critically important to cultivate the support and love of family and friends to encourage you, to walk alongside you, and to listen to you in the really tough days and weeks. There is also tremendous power in reaching out to friends from previous periods of your life who would gladly join in the fight for joy with you and restore hope. Social media is a wonderful tool to stay in contact with people across the globe. You would be surprised how much grace is contained in a few words from old friends. Their prayers on your behalf are a treasure. Some may even have traveled through the wilderness of suffering and have wisdom and a special strength to share with you.

So, to those who see hope as a four-letter word, I urge you to hold on to the vestigial scraps of hope that remains. I know how desperate and lost you can feel by going through years of suffering, loss, depression, and even betrayal. Each day a choice is made not to give up and to battle for life. These are withering days. But hold on! Ask people to help you. Ask God to rekindle the fire of hope in your soul. Ask Him to assure you of His presence with you. Look for the fingerprints of God in your life.

Hold on to the knowledge that God is with you, that He has a plan for your life, and that He will never leave you nor forsake you. Know that there are family and friends who love you and desire to support you. Embrace hope as a reliable source of light in the darkness, guiding you through the storms of life, and leading you to brighter days ahead.

# The Blessing of Adversity

In the depths of debilitation and pain, where every movement is a struggle and every breath a battle, life can quickly become a place of desolation and despondency. Simple tasks become Herculean feats, and every movement is accompanied by a symphony of discomfort. This physical burden can lead to exhaustion, frustration, and a sense of helplessness as we struggle to navigate a world that seems designed for the able-bodied.

Pain and debilitation also take a heavy toll on our emotional well-being. Chronic pain can lead to feelings of isolation, depression, and anxiety. The constant struggle to cope with physical discomfort can wear down our mental defenses, leaving us feeling vulnerable and overwhelmed. We may find ourselves questioning our worth, our purpose, and our place in the world.

But in the midst of suffering, we are reminded that God is close to us. In the front of our house is a ramp that was purchased and built for us by two families in our church. Every day, our ramp serves as a reminder of love, friendship, prayer, and support. In a very real sense, friends have made a way for us. Made a way into our home that reduces pain. Made a way that minimizes a risk to our safety, making it less likely to experience yet another fall. Made a way for others with physical infirmities to be welcomed into our home.

Ramps. Who would have thought it would have come to symbolize so much. Debilitation is indeed a great burden to bear. But debilitation can also be the avenue of tremendous blessing. Pain has a way of breaking down the barriers we erect around our hearts, allowing us to connect more deeply with the suffering of others. When we experience debilitation, we are able to empathize with those facing similar challenges, forging connections that transcend our own pain. In this way, our suffering can become a bridge to understanding and compassion.

When every movement is a struggle, the simplest tasks can become monumental achievements. In these moments, we learn to appreciate the small, often overlooked blessings of life: a ray of sunshine, a cool breeze, and the laughter of loved ones. Our pain teaches us to savor these moments, finding joy in the midst of struggle.

In the depths of our pain, we may find ourselves reaching out for comfort and meaning beyond the physical realm. This can be a time of profound spiritual awakening, as we grapple with questions of existence, purpose, and faith. Through our pain, we may discover a deeper connection to something greater than ourselves, finding comfort and strength that God is indeed with us, and He has always been with us. He has never left us or forsaken us.

Debilitation and pain are not easy companions, but they can be powerful teachers. In our darkest moments, we have the opportunity to break open, to grow, to empathize, to awaken, and to appreciate. These gifts, though hard-won, can transform our lives in ways we never imagined. So, let us not curse our pain, but instead, let us embrace it as a blessing in disguise, leading us on a journey of profound discovery and transformation.

# Feeling Stuck

Have you ever felt like you're stuck, trapped in a never-ending cycle, and unable to break free from the chains of inertia? Feeling stuck is like being in a dark tunnel with no light at the end, where each step forward feels like a struggle against an invisible force holding you back. It's a place of frustration, confusion, and sometimes despair, where the path ahead seems unclear and the way out feels impossible to find.

When you're stuck, it's not just a physical or mental state; it's an emotional and spiritual one, too. You may feel overwhelmed by a sense of helplessness, as if you're running in place while the world moves on without you. Doubt and fear may creep in, whispering that you're not good enough or that you'll never find a way out. It's a lonely place, where even in a crowd, you feel isolated and misunderstood. You wonder if God notices your hurt. Has even God left you in this uncomfortable place alone, making you find your own out all by yourself?

But here's the thing about feeling stuck: it's not permanent. It's a temporary state, a moment in time that will pass. And while it may feel like the end of the road, it's often the beginning of a new journey, one that can lead you to unexpected places and teach you valuable lessons along the way. So, what can you do when you find yourself in this place of stuckness?

The first step is to acknowledge and accept your feelings. Allow yourself to feel whatever emotions come up, whether it's frustration, sadness, or anger. Embrace these feelings with compassion and understanding, knowing that it's okay to not be okay.

Next, try to understand why you feel stuck. Is it because of external circumstances, such as a challenging work situation or a difficult relationship? Or is it internal, stemming from self-doubt or fear of the unknown? By identifying the root cause of your stuckness, you can begin to address it more effectively.

Once you have a better understanding of why you feel stuck, it's time to take action. Start by setting small, achievable goals for yourself. These goals should be specific, measurable, and realistic. By taking small steps towards your goals, you can build momentum and gradually break free from feeling stuck.

Seek support from others. Talk to friends, family, or a therapist about how you're feeling. Sometimes, just sharing your thoughts and feelings can provide a sense of relief and clarity. Additionally, seeking advice from others who have been in similar situations can provide valuable insights and perspectives.

Change your perspective. Instead of viewing feeling stuck as a negative experience, try to see it as an opportunity for growth and self-discovery. Use this time to reflect on your values, priorities, and goals in life. Sometimes, feeling stuck can lead you to new and exciting paths you never considered before.

Be patient and kind to yourself. Breaking free from feeling stuck takes time and effort. Celebrate small victories along the way, and don't be too hard on yourself if you experience setbacks. Remember, it's okay to ask for help and support when you need it.

Feeling stuck is not the end of your story; it's a chapter in the epic tale of your life. It's a moment of challenge that can be transformed into a triumph of the human spirit. Embrace this time of uncertainty as an opportunity for growth, for it is in the darkness that we discover our true strength and resilience. So, stand tall, face your fears, and step boldly into the light, for on the other side of stuckness lies a world of endless possibilities waiting to be explored.

# Developing Resilience

Resilience, that elusive quality that allows some to withstand life's harshest trials while others falter, is not merely a trait but a profound state of being. It is the art of bending without breaking, the ability to weather the fiercest storms and emerge stronger on the other side. To cultivate resilience is to embark on a journey of self-discovery, a quest to unlock the hidden depths of our innermost being.

Resilience, at its core, is a deeply spiritual journey. It is the art of surrendering to the flow of life, of trusting in a loving God to guide us through the darkest of times. It is the recognition that we are not alone in our struggles, that there is a Divine Presence that walks beside us, offering encouragement and strength. James reminds us: "Consider it pure joy, my brothers and sisters, whenever you face trials of many kinds, because you know that the testing of your faith produces perseverance." – James 1:2-3 (NIV)

At the heart of resilience lies a deep acceptance of life's impermanence and unpredictability. It is the recognition that change is the only constant, and that our ability to adapt to these changes determines our ability to thrive. This acceptance is not passive resignation but an active embrace of life in all its messy, unpredictable glory.

Resilience also requires us to cultivate a mindset of growth and possibility. It is about seeing challenges not as insurmountable obstacles but as opportunities for learning and growth. It is the belief that every setback is a steppingstone, every failure a lesson, and every hardship a chance to discover our own inner strength.

Building a strong, supportive community is another crucial aspect of resilience. It is the recognition that we are not meant to face life's challenges alone, that we are stronger together than we are apart. It is about surrounding ourselves with people who uplift and inspire us, who remind us of our own resilience when we falter.

Self-care is also essential for developing resilience. It is the recognition that our physical, emotional, and spiritual well-being are all interconnected, and that nurturing each of these aspects of ourselves is essential for building resilience. It is about prioritizing our own needs and taking the time to recharge and replenish ourselves so that we can face life's challenges with renewed vigor and determination.

Lastly, developing resilience requires us to cultivate a sense of purpose and meaning in our lives. It is the recognition that our struggles are not meaningless but are an integral part of our journey towards self-discovery and growth. It is about finding meaning in the midst of suffering and using that meaning to fuel our resilience and determination.

Developing resilience is a profound, transformative, and deeply spiritual journey that requires us to delve deep into the recesses of our own souls. At the core of resilience is a confidence in God's unfolding of His story, His plan for the tapestry of creation, including our individual life narratives.

Resilience is about embracing life in all its uncertainty and unpredictability and finding strength and meaning in the midst of adversity. It is a journey that requires courage, commitment, and above all, a deep belief in our own inner strength and our Eternal God.

Embrace the storms, for they are the crucible in which your character is forged. And know that, with God's grace and your unwavering spirit, you will emerge from every trial stronger, wiser, and more resilient than ever before.

# Is Love Enough?

Is love enough? It's a question that haunts us, especially when we stand at the edge of our deepest sorrows and most crushing defeats. When life shatters our dreams and leaves us gasping for breath, we wonder if love can truly be the balm that heals all wounds. Can love really sustain us when everything else falls apart?

In the glow of a wedding day, love feels invincible. The vows we exchange are filled with promises of eternal devotion, of standing by each other through thick and thin. But as the years go by, and life throws its harshest storms our way, we find ourselves grappling with the reality of love. When betrayal, loss, and disappointment knock on our door, we begin to question: Is love truly enough?

Jesus offers us a profound glimpse into the nature of love. His love wasn't confined to words or grand gestures alone; it was a love that bled and suffered, a love that bore the weight of the world's sins. In the Garden of Gethsemane, as He prayed in agony, we see a love that is willing to endure the unendurable. This is the love that calls us to go beyond ourselves, to give even when we feel we have nothing left to offer.

When my friend lost his child, his world collapsed. The pain was unbearable, a gaping wound that seemed impossible to heal. In his darkest moments, he questioned the sufficiency of love. Yet, it was love that surrounded him, held him up when he couldn't stand, wept with him, and whispered words of hope. Love didn't take away his pain, but it gave him the strength to face another day.

# The Tapestry of Life

Love is not always grandiose. Often, it's found in the small, quiet moments of life. It's in the hand that reaches out to comfort, the arms that embrace without asking for anything in return. It's in the silent prayers whispered in the dead of night, and in the steadfast presence of someone who simply stays. This kind of love might not fix everything, but it breathes life into our weary souls and gives us the courage to keep going.

There are times when love asks us to be vulnerable, to lay bare our deepest fears and wounds. It's terrifying to open up, to risk being hurt again. But in that vulnerability, we find a profound connection. Love requires courage—the courage to trust, to forgive, and to hope. It's through this courage that love becomes more than a feeling; it becomes a lifeline.

In our relationships, love is tested by everyday struggles and monumental challenges. The beauty of love is that it grows stronger in adversity. When we choose to love, even when it's hard, we reflect the love of Christ. His love was never easy, but it was always enough. It's this divine love that sustains us, that whispers to our hearts that we are not alone.

So, is love enough? Yes, love is enough—not because it erases all pain or solves every problem, but because it connects us to the heart of God. It is enough because it transforms us, gives us hope, and draws us closer to one another. Love is the most powerful force in the universe, a gift that keeps giving even in the darkest of times.

Let us cling to this love, let it fill our hearts and guide our actions. May we love deeply, fiercely, and unconditionally, trusting that in God's perfect love, we will find all we need.

# RECONCILIATION

Reconciliation is a profound act that bridges divides, heals wounds, and restores relationships. It is a process that requires humility, empathy, and courage. In our daily lives, we often encounter moments of tension, disagreement, or hurt with others. These moments can create distance and strain in our relationships, leaving us feeling disconnected and unsettled.

Our Lord in the Gospel of Matthew says: "So if you are offering your gift at the altar and there remember that your brother has something against you, leave your gift there before the altar and go. First, be reconciled to your brother, and then come and offer your gift" (Matt. 5:23-24). The call to reconciliation is a call to step beyond our pride and grievances and to seek peace and restoration. It is a call to emulate the love and forgiveness that God extends to us, even when we fall short.

Reconciliation is not always easy; it may require us to confront our own shortcomings, to listen with empathy, and to offer forgiveness even when it feels undeserved. In the midst of conflict and division, reconciliation offers a path forward—a path that leads to healing, understanding, and unity. It is a reminder that we are called to be peacemakers, to sow seeds of reconciliation in our relationships and communities.

As we go about our day, let us carry the spirit of reconciliation in our hearts. May we be guided by love, understanding, and forgiveness, seeking to mend what is broken and to build bridges of peace.

# You Are Enough!

In the quiet of the night, when the world settles into a hush, do you ever find your thoughts drifting to doubts and insecurities? Do you question your worth, wondering if you're truly enough? In a world that constantly pushes us to do more, work more, be more, have more, and be everything to everyone…it is very easy to believe that you are not enough, nor will you ever be enough.

The world often whispers, shouts, or insinuates that you are lacking, imperfect, or incomplete. But one truth… THE truth resounds: You are enough. This simple, profound statement carries a weight of reassurance that can transform the way you view yourself and your place in the world.

Life's pressures can sometimes make us feel inadequate. We may compare ourselves to others, measuring our worth against their achievements or appearances. But true worth isn't found in external accomplishments or validations. It's found within, in the depths of our being.

You are a unique creation of God, woven together with purpose and intention. You have been created as a gift by God to the people around you. Your talents, your quirks, and your dreams—they all contribute to the beautiful tapestry of who you are. There is no need to strive for perfection, for in your imperfections lies your uniqueness.

"You are enough" doesn't mean you have to be flawless or achieve some unattainable standard. It means recognizing your inherent worth, just as you are, with your strengths and weaknesses, your successes and failures. You are a unique masterpiece, a work in progress, constantly evolving and growing. And yet you are complete in Christ.

Embrace your flaws, for they are what make you human. Embrace your failures, for they are opportunities for growth. Embrace your journey, for it is uniquely yours. You are enough, not because of what you do or how you appear to others, but because of who you are at your core…a unique, special creation from the heart and mind of God.

Even in your weakest moments, when doubts cloud your mind and fears grip your heart, remember that you are enough. You are worthy of love, of acceptance, and of belonging. You don't need to earn these things; they are your birthright.

Understanding the truth that you are enough can free you from the tyranny of comparison and the pursuit of perfection. It allows you to live authentically, to celebrate your victories and learn from your mistakes, without being weighed down by unrealistic expectations.

So, let go of the need to prove yourself to others. Let go of the fear of not measuring up. Instead, embrace the truth that you are enough, just as you are. Embrace the love that surrounds you, the love that sees you for who you truly are and accepts you without judgment.

In the grand scheme of life, what truly matters is not how others perceive you, but how you perceive yourself. So, see yourself through the eyes of God. See yourself through eyes of kindness and compassion. See yourself as the unique and valuable individual that you are. You are enough, my friend. Always remember that.

# WORTHY OF LOVE

In life's intricate tapestry, we often find ourselves entwined in a web of self-perception, a lens through which we view the world and ourselves. This lens, shaped by our experiences, upbringing, and inner dialogue, influences how we receive love. Yet, what if this lens is flawed, tainted by doubts and insecurities, leading us to believe we deserve less than we truly do?

Many people only accept the love they think they deserve, a poignant realization that speaks to the heart of our self-worth. We settle for morsels of affection, crumbs of kindness, when in reality, we are deserving of a feast of love and acceptance.

At times, this belief stems from past wounds, echoes of rejection, or abandonment that whisper lies about our worthiness. We internalize these falsehoods, building walls around our hearts, fearing that if others truly knew us, they would not love us. Yet, these walls only serve to block the flow of love into our lives, leaving us parched in a desert of our own making.

But there is hope. For just as we have internalized these beliefs, so too can we unlearn them. We can rewrite the script of our self-worth, embracing the truth that we are worthy of love simply because we exist. We need not perform or achieve to earn love; it is our birthright.

In the quiet moments of reflection, we can begin to dismantle these walls, brick by brick, replacing them with windows that allow the light of love to shine in. We can choose to surround ourselves with people who see us as we truly are, who reflect back to us the love and value we possess. We can realign our thinking when we understand that God loves us supremely, unconditionally, and sacrificially. There is nothing we can do to make God love us more or less.

Ultimately, accepting the love we truly deserve is an act of courage, a willingness to step into our true selves, unmasked and unafraid. It is a declaration that we are enough, just as we are, worthy of love in its purest form.

So, let us open our hearts to receive love in all its forms, for in doing so, we not only enrich our own lives, but also create a ripple effect of love that touches all those around us.

# Cultivating Hope

How can we infuse hope in our lives and the lives of other people? Infusing our lives with hope is a deeply personal and spiritual journey that requires us to confront our fears, uncertainties, and doubts.

At the core of hope is a profound sense of trust—in ourselves, in others, and in the goodness of God. It's about believing that no matter how dire the circumstances may seem, there is a personal, loving God Who is guiding us towards a brighter future. This trust is not blind faith but a conscious choice to see the world through a lens of possibility rather than limitation. Our hope is founded squarely in our Creator, trusting that He desires to prosper us, to give us hope and a future.

To cultivate hope, we must also confront our fears of failure and disappointment. It's natural to be afraid of putting ourselves out there, of taking risks, and of daring to dream big. But hope calls us to embrace these fears and to see them not as obstacles but as steppingstones on the path to growth and fulfillment.

Infusing our lives with hope requires us to confront our own mortality and impermanence. It's about recognizing the fleeting nature of life and finding meaning and purpose in the face of uncertainty. This recognition can be both daunting and liberating, as it reminds us to cherish each moment and to live authentically, in alignment with our deepest values and aspirations.

Conveying hope to others is an act of profound vulnerability and empathy. It's about opening our hearts to the pain and suffering of

# The Tapestry of Life

others and offering them a glimmer of light in their darkest moments. This requires us to set aside our own fears and insecurities and to be fully present for those in need, offering them not just words of comfort but a genuine connection born out of shared humanity. We refrain from offering empty platitudes or false promises of a better tomorrow; it is about bearing witness to the struggles of our fellow human beings with empathy and compassion. It is about standing in solidarity with those who are suffering and offering a hand to lift them up when they falter. It is about being light in a world that too often feels shrouded in darkness, and inspiring others to find hope within themselves

Ultimately, infusing our lives with hope is an ongoing process—one that requires courage, resilience, and a willingness to embrace the full spectrum of human experience. It's about acknowledging the darkness within us and around us but refusing to be consumed by it. Instead, it's about choosing to see the beauty, the goodness, and the infinite possibilities that exist in every moment, no matter how challenging or bleak the circumstances may seem.

Infusing our lives with hope is a deeply spiritual and transformative journey that calls us to confront our fears, uncertainties, and doubts. It's about trusting in the inherent goodness of God and embracing the full spectrum of human experience with courage and resilience. As we navigate this journey, let us remember that hope is not just a fleeting emotion but a profound state of being—one that empowers us to live fully, love deeply, and create a more compassionate and hopeful world for all.

# The Wilderness of Suffering

The wilderness of suffering is a desolate place, where the harsh winds of pain and despair can leave us feeling lost and alone. The wilderness of suffering is a sorrowful place that many of us find ourselves in at some point in our lives. It is a place that withers souls, where the landscape of our hearts is parched with discomfort, and our spirits are weary from the journey. In the midst of this wilderness, it can be easy to lose sight of God's presence, to doubt His goodness and His plan for us. Then we read this passage from Isaiah 55:

"For my thoughts are not your thoughts, neither are your ways my ways," declares the Lord. "As the heavens are higher than the earth, so are my ways higher than your ways and my thoughts than your thoughts."–Isaiah 55:8-9

In the midst of our suffering, we are reminded that God's thoughts are not our thoughts, and His ways are not our ways. His ways are higher, His thoughts more profound than we can ever imagine. In the wilderness of suffering, we are called to trust in God's higher ways, to believe that He is at work in ways that we cannot see or understand.

Like the Israelites wandering in the desert, we may feel lost and alone in our suffering. We may wonder why God has led us into this wilderness, and why He doesn't lead us out. In the face of suffering, we are called to remember that God's ways are not our ways. He sees the bigger picture, the purpose behind our suffering that may be hidden from our eyes.

In the wilderness of suffering, we are invited to surrender our doubts and fears to God, trusting that His ways are perfect. We are called to trust in His wisdom and His plan for our lives, even when we cannot see the path ahead. As we do, we may find that the wilderness is not a place of abandonment, but a place of transformation, where our suffering becomes a means through which God's glory is revealed.

As we meditate on this passage from Isaiah, let us be reminded that our suffering is not in vain. God is still with us. He is still a loving, faithful, and unimaginably good God. He has not abandoned us. God is at work in ways that we cannot see, using our pain to bring about His purposes. May we find comfort in knowing that we serve a God whose thoughts are higher than our thoughts, and whose ways are higher than our ways.

Prayer:

Heavenly Father, in the midst of the wilderness of suffering, help us to trust in Your higher ways. Give us the faith to believe that You are at work in ways that we cannot see, using these times of adversity for Your glory. May we surrender our doubts and fears to You, trusting that Your ways are perfect.

Amen.

# THE INNER SANCTUM OF OUR SOULS

In the depths of our being, where the light of day struggles to reach, lie the most intimate battles we face. These are the struggles we dare not speak of, the pains we hide behind smiles, and the wounds we dress in solitude.

In the quiet of the night, when the world sleeps, these struggles awaken, demanding attention. They whisper in our ears, echoing the ache in our hearts, and we are left to wrestle with them in the darkness.

In the sanctum of our souls, we carry burdens known only to us. They are intensely private struggles, veiled from the world, and shaping our journey in profound ways. They test our resilience, challenge our faith, and reveal the depths of our strength.

Intensely private struggles come in many forms. It could be the silent fight against a relentless illness, the daily battle with self-doubt and insecurity, a troubled marital relationship, or the hidden pain of past traumas. Such persistent struggles can be isolating, making us feel misunderstood and alone.

These are the struggles that leave no physical scars but weigh heavily on the soul. Yet, it's precisely in these moments of solitude that grace can be found. It's the grace to acknowledge our vulnerabilities, to accept our imperfections, and to find strength in our weaknesses. It's the grace to forgive ourselves for not being perfect, for not having it all together.

## The Tapestry of Life

In the depths of our struggles, we often discover a reservoir of resilience we never knew we had. It's a resilience born out of necessity, a survival instinct that pushes us forward even when every fiber of our being wants to give up.

It's okay to struggle. It's okay to feel overwhelmed. It's okay to not have all the answers. In these moments, it's important to remember that you are not alone. There is grace in reaching out for help, in sharing your burden with God and those you trust. You are already accepted and loved by God. You do not need to fight for His acceptance. The Spirit of God walks with you (Romans 8).

May you find solace in the knowledge that your struggles do not define you. They are a part of your story, but they are not the whole story. You are stronger than you know, and you are worthy of love and compassion, especially from yourself.

Take a moment today to acknowledge your silent struggles. Offer yourself the same grace and understanding you would offer a dear friend. You are deserving of kindness, especially from yourself.

# Interludes of Vulnerability

In the sanctuary of our hearts, there are chambers seldom opened, where our deepest battles are fought in silence. These intensely private personal struggles, shrouded in the veil of solitude, can weigh heavy on our souls, casting shadows even in the brightest of days.

In these sacred sanctuaries of struggle, we often find ourselves wrestling with shadows that others cannot perceive. These are the struggles that defy easy explanation, the pains that elude description, and the burdens that seem too heavy to bear. They are the silent cries for help that echo within us, the unseen tears that fall in solitude, and the wounds that scar our souls.

In those moments when the weight feels unbearable and the darkness threatens to engulf us, it's easy to believe we are alone in our struggles. Yet, it is precisely in these depths that we find the hand of the Divine, gently guiding us towards the light.

Like a beacon in the night, hope flickers amidst the darkness, reminding us that even in our most private struggles, we are never truly alone. For God, our Creator, dwells within us, intimately acquainted with every ache, every doubt, and every tear that falls unseen.

It's in the quiet moments of reflection and prayer that we can begin to unravel the knots of our inner turmoil, laying bare our vulnerabilities before the One who sees and understands all. In this sacred exchange of trust, we find comfort in knowing that our struggles need not to be carried in isolation.

In these interludes of profound vulnerability, we are invited to embrace our humanity in its entirety—to acknowledge our weaknesses, our fears, our doubts, and to find within them the seeds of transformation. For it is only by facing our struggles head-on, by embracing them as integral parts of who we are, that we can begin to find healing and wholeness.

Though the journey through private struggles may be fraught with uncertainty and pain, it is also a path illuminated by grace. It is through our brokenness that the light of compassion and empathy shines brightest, bridging the chasm between our hearts and those of others who may be silently wrestling with their own demons.

As we navigate the labyrinth of our innermost fears and insecurities, let us not forget that vulnerability is not a sign of weakness, but rather a testament to the resilience of the human spirit. It is through our willingness to confront our private struggles with courage and authenticity that we find the strength to rise above them, transformed by the healing power of love.

So, dear friend, if you find yourself engulfed in the depths of private struggles, know that you are seen, you are heard, and you are held in the embrace of Divine love. May you find comfort in the knowledge that your journey, though intensely personal, is also a sacred pilgrimage towards wholeness and restoration.

# The Sacred Space of Accountability

In the corridors of our minds, a silent battle often wages—a struggle between two narratives: "it's all my fault" versus "it's everyone else's fault." It's a familiar dichotomy, one that often emerges in moments of adversity, when the weight of responsibility presses upon us.

In moments of self-doubt and vulnerability, it's easy to succumb to the belief that every misstep, every stumble, is solely our own doing. We carry the burden of blame upon our shoulders, internalizing it until it becomes an inseparable part of our identity. We dwell on our shortcomings, replaying past mistakes like a broken record, convinced that we alone are to blame for our perceived failures.

Conversely, there are times when we seek relief in shifting the blame outward, deflecting responsibility onto others. We point fingers, assigning fault to external circumstances, individuals, or forces beyond our control. In doing so, we relinquish agency, surrendering to the notion that we are mere pawns in the grand tapestry of life, victims of circumstance rather than active participants in our own destiny.

Yet, in the midst of this internal tug-of-war, there lies a path of liberation—a path illuminated by the light of accountability. True accountability does not entail shouldering the entirety of the blame nor absolving ourselves of all responsibility. Rather, it involves embracing the complexity of our experiences, acknowledging our role in shaping them while recognizing the myriad factors that influence our journey.

At its core, accountability is an act of courage—a willingness to confront our vulnerabilities, acknowledge our imperfections, and strive for growth. It requires humility, the humility to admit when we've erred, to seek forgiveness, and to learn from our mistakes. It also demands empathy, the ability to extend grace not only to ourselves but to others, understanding that we are all navigating the labyrinth of life to the best of our abilities.

In the sacred space of accountability, we discover a profound truth: that our worth is not contingent upon our perceived successes or failures, but on the authenticity of our journey—the courage to confront our shadows, the resilience to rise from the ashes, and the grace to walk alongside others with humility and compassion.

So, let us embrace accountability as a sacred covenant—a testament to our humanity, our interconnectedness, and our capacity for growth. For in the crucible of accountability, we find not condemnation, but liberation—a pathway to wholeness, authenticity, and grace.

# Infusing Joy

Our relationships are like gardens, requiring care and attention to flourish. Just as a garden needs water and sunlight to thrive, our relationships need joy to grow and bloom. Infusing joy into our relationships is a choice—a conscious decision to cultivate love and happiness in our interactions with others.

One way to infuse joy into our relationships is through gratitude. Taking time to appreciate the people in our lives and the blessings they bring can transform our relationships from mundane to extraordinary. When we express gratitude, we not only uplift others but also uplift ourselves, creating a positive and joyful atmosphere that nurtures love and connection.

Another way to infuse joy into our relationships is through acts of kindness and generosity. Simple gestures, such as a kind word, a thoughtful gesture, or a small gift, can brighten someone's day and strengthen the bond between us. When we give freely and without expectation, we create a ripple effect of joy that enriches our relationships and brings us closer together.

Infusing joy into our relationships also requires us to be present and engaged. In our fast-paced world, it's easy to get caught up in our own thoughts and distractions, but true joy in relationships comes from being fully present with the people we care about. When we listen attentively, show empathy, and share in both the joys and sorrows of others, we deepen our connections and create lasting memories of love and joy.

Ultimately, infusing joy into our relationships is about choosing love over fear, kindness over indifference, and gratitude over entitlement. It is about recognizing the precious gift of each moment we have with others and cherishing the opportunity to share our lives with them.

Today, let us make a commitment to infuse joy into our relationships. Let us choose to be grateful, to be kind, and to be present with the people we love. In doing so, we not only enrich our own lives but also bring light and love into the lives of others.

# Radical Acceptance

In a world that often values perfection and flawlessness, it can be challenging to embrace our own imperfections, and the flaws of others. We may feel pressure to meet unrealistic standards or to hide our weaknesses. However, as followers of Christ, we are called to view imperfection through a different lens–the lens of grace.

In our journey of faith, we are called to love one another deeply and unconditionally, just as our Creator loves us. This love is not superficial or conditional; it is transformative, capable of changing hearts and lives. It is a love that sees beyond our imperfections and flaws, accepting us as we are.

God's love for us is the perfect example of this transformative love. Despite knowing all of our shortcomings, He loves us unconditionally. His love is not based on our performance or our ability to meet certain standards. Instead, it is a love that embraces us in our brokenness, offering us grace and forgiveness.

As followers of Christ, we are called to extend this same love to others. This means accepting people as they are, with all their imperfections and flaws. It means making room for mistakes, forgiving freely, and offering grace generously. It means seeing the potential for transformation in every person we meet. "Above all, love each other deeply, because love covers over a multitude of sins." (I Peter 4:8)

Transformative love does not mean condoning sin or overlooking wrongdoing. It means loving the person while hating the sin, just as God does. It means recognizing that we are all on a journey of growth and change, and that we all need grace along the way.

Jesus exemplified this kind of radical acceptance in His ministry. He welcomed sinners and outcasts, showing them love and compassion. He saw beyond their flaws to the beauty of their souls. As His followers, we are called to do the same.

When we make room for imperfection in our relationships, we create space for authenticity and vulnerability. We allow others to be themselves, without fear of judgment or rejection. This kind of acceptance can be transformative, leading to deeper, more meaningful connections.

Today, let us strive to love one another deeply and unconditionally, just as God loves us. Let us make room for imperfections and flaws, knowing that it is through love that true transformation occurs. May our love be a light in the darkness, a beacon of hope to all who are in need.

Prayer:

Heavenly Father, thank You for Your unconditional love and acceptance. Help us to love one another deeply, just as You love us. Teach us to make room for imperfections and flaws, and to extend grace and forgiveness to all. In Jesus' name, Amen.

# Facing Unjust Treatment

Life often presents us with situations where we are treated unjustly. Whether it's at work, in our communities, or even within our families, unfair treatment can leave us feeling hurt, frustrated, and angry. It can be tempting to retaliate, to seek revenge, or to simply wallow in self-pity. However, as followers of Christ, we are called to respond differently.

Jesus faced some of the most unfair treatment imaginable. He was betrayed by one of His closest friends, denied by another, and ultimately crucified despite being innocent. Yet, in the face of such injustice, He responded with love, forgiveness, and grace. He taught us to turn the other cheek, to love our enemies, and to pray for those who persecute us.

This is not an easy command to follow. Betrayal, the silence of your friends when they see you being mistreated, and character assassination…situations like these wound us deeply. It requires us to set aside our pride, our desire for vengeance, and our need to be understood. Instead, we are called to trust in God's justice, to rely on His strength, and to emulate Christ's example of love and forgiveness.

When we are treated unfairly, we can find comfort in knowing that we are not alone. Jesus understands our pain, and He walks beside us, offering us His peace and His strength. Through prayer, we can find the courage to forgive those who have wronged us, to let go of our anger, and to trust in God's plan for justice. Matthew 5:44 encourages us to go a significant step farther, Jesus instructing us, "But I say to you, Love your enemies and pray for those who persecute you."

Today, if you are facing unfair treatment, may you turn to Jesus. Seek His guidance, His comfort, and His peace. Remember that He is with you always, and He will never leave you nor forsake you. May His love fill your heart, and may His grace empower you to respond with kindness and forgiveness, even in the face of injustice.

# Embracing our Uniqueness

In the vast canvas of the universe, each soul is a stroke of divine artistry, painted with unique hues and textures. You are a masterpiece in your own right, crafted with precision and purpose. Your uniqueness is not a flaw but a feature, a testament to the boundless creativity of the Creator.

In a world that often pressures us to conform, it's easy to forget the beauty of our uniqueness. Each of us is a masterpiece, intricately designed by a loving Creator. Psalm 139:14 reminds us that, "I praise you because I am fearfully and wonderfully made; your works are wonderful, I know that full well." This means that every detail of our being is intentionally crafted by God's hand.

Consider for a moment the complexity of a snowflake or the intricacy of a spider's web. Just as these creations are uniquely formed, so are we. Our personalities, talents, and even our imperfections are part of a divine design.

Embracing your uniqueness is not about seeking validation from others or conforming to societal standards. It is about recognizing and celebrating the qualities that make you one-of-a-kind. Your journey is yours alone, and the path you walk has never been tread on by another.

Embracing our uniqueness means celebrating our differences and recognizing the value we bring to the world. It's about being comfortable in our own skin and using our gifts to uplift and inspire

THE TAPESTRY OF LIFE

others. When we fully grasp the depth of God's love for us, we can embrace our uniqueness with confidence and joy.

You are a rare gem, a fresh thought from God, a reflection of divine love and creativity. Embrace your uniqueness, for it is the key to unlocking your truest self and fulfilling your purpose in this world. So, today, take a moment to reflect on the ways in which you are uniquely designed. Give thanks for the traits that make you who you are, knowing that you are a special creation, loved deeply by your Creator. As you go about your day, let your light shine brightly, knowing that you are fearfully and wonderfully made.

Prayer:

Dear Lord, thank You for creating me in Your image and for designing me with purpose and intention. Help me to embrace my uniqueness and to use my gifts to glorify You. Amen.

# Yearning for Connection

In the depths of our souls, there is a longing for something more, something beyond the surface of life. It is a longing for connection—with ourselves, with others, and with God. This longing is echoed in the words of the psalmist who wrote, "Deep calls to deep in the roar of your waterfalls; all your waves and breakers have swept over me" (Psalm 42:7).

These words remind us that there is a depth to life that goes beyond what we can see and touch. It is a depth that calls out to us, inviting us to peel back the mysteries of existence, and to explore the depths of our own souls.

When we heed this call, we open ourselves up to a world of beauty, wonder, and meaning that transcends the ordinary. We begin to see the world with new eyes, to hear the world with new ears, and to feel the world with a new heart.

In the deepest recesses of our souls, there is a yearning for connection—a longing to be united with something greater than ourselves. This longing is like a deep well within us, calling out to the deep well of creation and to the deep well of each other, seeking to be filled, seeking to be understood, and seeking to be one.

When we look out at the world around us, we see the beauty of creation—the mountains, the oceans, and the forests—all created with a depth and intricacy that reflects the depth and intricacy of our own souls. In the beauty of creation, we see the handiwork of

# The Tapestry of Life

our Creator and we feel a visceral calling within us to connect, to commune, and to be in relationship with all that is.

But the call of the deep is not just about our connection to creation—it is also about our connection to each other. Each person we encounter bears the Image of God, a mirror that shows us aspects of ourselves that we may not have seen before. When we take the time to truly listen to each other, to truly see each other, we are answering the call of the deep, allowing our souls to connect in a way that is profound and transformative.

When we heed the call of the deep, we open ourselves up to a resonate understanding of ourselves and of the world around us. We see that we are not separate, but interconnected, woven together in a tapestry of life that is both beautiful and complex.

Today, let us heed the call of the deep. Let us take a moment to connect—with creation, with each other, and with God. And may we be filled with a deep sense of peace and belonging, knowing that we are part of something greater than ourselves, knowing that we are all connected in the deep.

# TRUE BEAUTY

In our fast-paced world, beauty is often associated with the grand and the magnificent—the breathtaking sunsets, the majestic mountains, and the stunning works of art. We are taught to seek beauty in the extraordinary, in the things that stand out and command our attention.

But what if true beauty lies not only in the grand and the magnificent, but in the quiet and the overlooked? What if it is found not in the spotlight, but in the shadows, waiting to be discovered by those who are willing to look a little deeper?

In our quest for beauty, we often seek it in the external world—in the grandeur of nature, the creativity of art, and the symmetry of architecture. Yet, there is a beauty that lies within us, waiting to be discovered and embraced.

True beauty is not found in outward appearances, but in the depths of the heart. It is in the qualities of gratitude, kindness, compassion, and forgiveness that the true beauty of a person is revealed.

Gratitude is a powerful force that can transform our lives. When we approach each day with a grateful heart, we open ourselves up to the beauty and abundance that surrounds us. Even in the midst of difficulties, there is always something to be grateful for—a kind word, a beautiful sunset, and a moment of peace.

Kindness is another beautiful quality that can brighten someone's day and bring joy to the world. A simple act of kindness, whether it's a smile, a helping hand, or a kind word, can have a ripple effect, spreading love and compassion to those around us.

Compassion is the ability to empathize with others and show them love and understanding. When we approach others with compassion, we are able to see beyond their outward appearance or actions and recognize the beauty within them.

Forgiveness is perhaps the most beautiful of all. It is the act of letting go of resentment and anger, and choosing to see the humanity in others. When we forgive, we free ourselves from the burden of bitterness and allow love to heal our hearts.

Today, let us cultivate these qualities in our hearts. Let us approach each day with gratitude, showing kindness to others, and practicing compassion and forgiveness. In doing so, may we reveal the true beauty that lies within us, in others, and may we be a beacon of light and love in the world.

# The Call to Love Radically

Jesus loved people. He never had a condition, never a prerequisite, and no requirement that was necessary before He loved people. Even when He was abandoned, betrayed, and cursed by everyone, Jesus loved. He loved first. He loved people just the way they were. Everyone. No exceptions.

The love of Jesus is a powerful, awe-inspiring force that defies human logic. Picture Jesus standing in the midst of a crowd, His eyes filled with compassion, and His heart overflowing with love for each person He encounters. There is no judgment in His gaze, no hesitation in His touch. His love is pure, unconditional, and all-encompassing. It reaches out to the outcast, the sinner, the broken, and the lost. He sees beyond their flaws and failures, embracing them with open arms.

In stark contrast, we often find ourselves placing conditions on our love. Are there conditions or prerequisites we have before we deem a person "worthy" of our love? Do we love some people, but withhold it from others? Why? What criteria do we use to justify such decisions? Perhaps it's because we fear vulnerability, or we've been hurt before. Maybe it's because we've been taught to love those who are like us and to distance ourselves from those who are different. Whatever the reason, these barriers prevent us from experiencing the fullness of the love that Jesus calls us to.

In a world full of people who have a profound longing, a visceral need to be loved…how can we expand our capacity to love? Imagine the impact if we chose to love with the same radical, unreserved love that Jesus demonstrated. A love that doesn't wait for the other person to be worthy but sees their worth simply because they are a child of God. A love that breaks down walls and bridges divides. It starts with small, intentional acts of kindness. A smile to a stranger, a listening ear to a friend in need, and a helping hand to someone struggling. It means being present, truly seeing the people around us, and responding with compassion.

Even when we are treated poorly, can we respond with love and kindness? This is perhaps the greatest test of our commitment to follow Jesus' example. When we are hurt, our natural response is to build walls, to protect ourselves from further pain. But Jesus calls us to a higher standard. "But I tell you, love your enemies and pray for those who persecute you" (Matthew 5:44). It's in these moments of vulnerability that our love can shine the brightest, reflecting the unconditional love that Jesus has for us.

Loving others is a powerful way to make each of our little corners of the world a better place. Imagine the impact if each of us committed to loving as Jesus did, without conditions or prerequisites. The ripple effect of such love can transform families, communities, and nations. It can make an unbelievable difference to a hurting person, battered and broken by the world.

Offer safe harbor, a haven of healing, and rest to the people in your sphere of life, by being gentle, kind, and loving. Be a beacon of hope in the midst of despair, a source of comfort in times of trouble. Remember, it is through our love that others can glimpse the heart of God. As we extend grace, kindness, and love, we become living testimonies of Jesus' love—a love that changes lives, heals wounds, and brings about true peace.

Let us commit to loving boldly, radically, and unconditionally, just as Jesus loves us. In doing so, we not only honor Him but also bring His light into a world desperately in need of love.

# HOLY INEFFICIENCY

In our fast-paced world, efficiency is often praised as a virtue. We strive to do more in less time, to streamline our processes, and to maximize our productivity. Yet, there are moments when efficiency falls short, when our best-laid plans crumble, and we're left feeling frustrated and defeated. It's in these moments that we're invited to embrace the concept of "holy inefficiency." This idea challenges our cultural obsession with efficiency and productivity, instead inviting us to embrace the mystery and wonder of God's ways.

Holy inefficiency invites us to trust in God's timing and His ways, even when they seem inefficient or illogical to us. It challenges us to surrender our need for control and to embrace the mystery of God's plans.

Throughout the Bible, we encounter stories of God working in ways that seem inefficient by human standards. Consider the story of the Israelites wandering in the wilderness for forty years before entering the Promised Land. To the Israelites, it may have seemed like a wasted journey, but God was using that time to refine and prepare them for what lay ahead.

Jesus likened the kingdom of God to a mustard seed, which is one of the smallest seeds, yet grows into a large tree. This image reminds us that God's work often starts small and is seemingly insignificant but can grow into something beautiful and impactful beyond our imagination.

Similarly, in the New Testament, Jesus often took His time to minister to individuals, even when it seemed impractical or inefficient.

# The Tapestry of Life

In the story of Lazarus' death, Jesus deliberately delayed His arrival, allowing Lazarus to die and be buried for four days before raising him from the dead. To the disciples, this delay may have seemed unnecessary, but Jesus used it to demonstrate His power over death and to deepen their faith.

In our own lives, we may experience seasons of waiting, delay, or apparent inefficiency. We may question why God seems to be taking His time or why His ways don't align with our plans. But in those moments, let's remember that God's timing is perfect, and His ways are higher than ours.

In our fast-paced world, we can easily become discouraged when our efforts seem small or ineffective. We may question the value of our faith or feel inadequate compared to others. However, holy inefficiency teaches us to trust in God's timing and methods, even when they seem slow or unconventional.

Holy inefficiency invites us to trust in God's providence and surrender our need for control. It reminds us that God is not bound by human constraints of time, or efficiency, but works according to His perfect will and purposes.

Instead of resisting the delays or detours in our journey, let's embrace them as opportunities for growth, faith, and dependence on God. Let's trust that, even in the midst of seeming inefficiency, God is at work, weaving together the threads of our lives into a beautiful tapestry of His grace and redemption.

As we surrender our plans and agendas to God, may we find peace in knowing that His ways are always for our ultimate good and His glory, even if they may seem inefficient from our limited perspective.

When you feel your faith faltering, remember that God's ways are not our ways. His plans are often mysterious and beyond our understanding. Embrace the small acts of faithfulness in your life, trusting that God can use them to bring about His purposes in ways you may never see or comprehend.

# The Journey Through Suffering

In times of suffering, our faith can be tested in ways we never imagined. It's natural to hope that our faith will emerge from suffering intact and whole, but the reality is that the journey through suffering can leave us feeling broken and uncertain.

Suffering has a way of challenging our faith, often leaving us feeling battered and worn. When we experience suffering, whether physical, emotional, or spiritual, it can deeply shake our faith. We may question why God allows such pain and hardship in our lives. We may find ourselves questioning God's goodness or struggling to make sense of the pain we are experiencing. As we traverse the wilderness of suffering, it's important to remember that our faith is not meant to remain intact and whole through suffering; rather, it is meant to be transformed and deepened.

In the book of Job, we see a man who experienced immense suffering yet remained faithful to God. Job's story reminds us that suffering does not necessarily result in a stronger or more resilient faith. Instead, it can leave us feeling raw and vulnerable, unsure of where to turn, or how to make sense of our pain.

Please understand that our faith is not measured by our ability to endure suffering with unwavering certainty. Rather, it's about our willingness to trust God even when we don't understand His ways. As the psalmist writes in Psalm 34:18, "The Lord is close to the brokenhearted and saves those who are crushed in spirit." God is not distant or indifferent to our suffering; He is with us in the midst of it, offering us comfort and hope.

Our faith may not come through suffering intact and whole, but that doesn't mean it is lost. Suffering has a way of stripping away the superficial and revealing the true depth of our faith. It is in these moments of brokenness that we can experience God's grace in a profound and transformative way.

In 2 Corinthians 4:8-9, the apostle Paul writes, "We are hard pressed on every side, but not crushed; perplexed, but not in despair; persecuted, but not abandoned; struck down, but not destroyed." These words remind us that while we may face suffering and trials, our faith can endure.

But not all stories of suffering end with such a clear resolution. Sometimes, despite our prayers and our best efforts, the suffering persists. In the midst of such profound misery, it can feel like our faith is slipping away, leaving us feeling abandoned and alone. It's okay to acknowledge these feelings, to cry out to God in our pain and confusion…God remains faithful to us even when our faith is fleeting and failing.

So, if you find yourself in the midst of suffering and your faith feels fragile and uncertain, know that you are not alone. God is with you, and He is faithful. Trust in His love and His plan, even when it's hard, and allow Him to heal and restore your faith in His timing and His way.

# Moments of Grandeur

In the midst of life's trials and tribulations, it's easy to become ensnared by the weight of our burdens. Yet, in these moments of despair, there exists a profound remedy: the grandeur of creation.

When we find ourselves wounded and weary, it's essential to seek solace in the vastness of nature. Whether it be the majestic peaks of towering mountains, the endless expanse of the ocean's horizon, or the serene beauty of a sunset painting the sky in hues of gold and crimson, nature's grandeur speaks to the depths of our souls, offering healing and renewal.

In the presence of such magnificence, our troubles seem insignificant, dwarfed by the sheer magnitude of creation. We are reminded that we are but small parts of a much larger, awe-inspiring tapestry woven by the hand of the God. In this realization, we find comfort and perspective, understanding that our struggles are but fleeting moments in the grand arc of eternity.

Moreover, the grandeur of creation serves as a tangible reminder of God's presence and providence in our lives. Just as the sun rises faithfully each morning and the stars twinkle overhead in the night sky, so too does God's love and grace shine upon us, unwavering and constant. In the face of adversity, we can take refuge in the knowledge that we are held in the palm of His hand, surrounded by His boundless love.

As we immerse ourselves in the splendor of nature's grandeur, we are invited to release our burdens and surrender to the peace that surpasses all understanding. In the stillness of the wilderness or the roar of the ocean's waves, we discover a sanctuary for our weary souls, a sacred space where healing begins, and hope is restored.

Through experiencing grandeur, we are invited to surrender our burdens and open our hearts to the possibility of healing. It is a gentle reminder that beauty exists even in the midst of pain, and that joy can be found in the most unexpected places. So let us seek out moments of grandeur, allowing them to soothe our wounded hearts and lift our spirits towards the heavens. For in the presence of grandeur, healing begins, and hope is renewed. In its majesty, may we find the strength to persevere, the courage to face our trials, and the faith to trust in God's unfailing goodness.

# Embrace the Cross

The most challenging aspect of the Christian experience lies in the call to embrace the cross – to follow in the footsteps of Christ, bearing our own burdens, and sacrificing our own desires for the sake of love and service. It is a journey fraught with difficulty and discomfort, yet it is also the path to true discipleship and spiritual fulfillment.

At the heart of the Christian faith is the paradox of the cross – a symbol of suffering and redemption, of death and new life. Jesus Himself exemplified this paradox through His sacrificial death on the cross, offering Himself as a ransom for the sins of humanity. He calls us to take up our own crosses and follow Him, surrendering our will to the will of God and embracing the challenges and trials that come our way.

The most challenging aspect of the Christian experience is not merely enduring suffering or facing adversity, but rather doing so with a spirit of humility, grace, and love. It is easy to become discouraged or resentful in the face of hardship, to question God's goodness or to turn inward in self-pity. Yet, it is precisely in these moments that our faith is tested, and our character is refined.

In the words of the apostle Paul, "I have been crucified with Christ and I no longer live, but Christ lives in me. The life I now live in the body, I live by faith in the Son of God, who loved me and gave Himself for me" (Galatians 2:20, NIV). As followers of Christ, we are called to die to our own selfish ambitions and desires, and to live for the glory of God and the good of others.

Embracing the cross is not merely an abstract theological concept; it is a daily, lived reality that challenges us to die to ourselves and to take up our crosses daily. It is in the moments of trial, temptation, and adversity that we are called to embody the sacrificial love of Christ, even when it seems counterintuitive or contrary to our natural inclinations.

The journey of embracing the cross is not an easy one, but it is a journey filled with purpose, meaning, and ultimately, hope. It is a journey of transformation – of becoming more like Christ in our thoughts, words, and actions. And though the road may be steep, and the way may be narrow, we can take comfort in the knowledge that we do not walk alone – for Christ walks with us, carrying us through the darkest valleys and leading us into the light of His love.

So, let us not shrink back from the challenges that come our way, but instead, let us embrace them with courage and faith, knowing that even in the midst of our struggles, God is at work, weaving beauty from ashes and transforming our pain into purpose. As we take up our cross and follow Jesus, may we find strength in His presence, hope in His promises, and joy in the knowledge that our suffering is never in vain.

# The Depths of Desolation

In the depths of our existence, there are moments when the soul encounters desolation—times when the world seems bleak, and the light of hope flickers dimly. It's in these moments of despair that we find ourselves questioning our purpose, our worth, and even the existence of divine love. Soul desolation can come in many forms—loss, disappointment, betrayal, or simply the weariness of life's struggles. It's a place where doubts and fears can take root, threatening to overshadow the light of faith.

Soul desolation is a profound state of emptiness and spiritual despair that permeates the core of one's being. It is a barren landscape of the heart, where the vibrant colors of hope and faith have faded into shades of gray. In this desolate terrain, there is a profound sense of isolation, as if one is traversing a vast and lonely wilderness with no end in sight.

At the heart of soul desolation lies a deep sense of disconnection — from oneself, from others, and from our Creator. It is a feeling of being adrift in a sea of uncertainty, with no guidance or comfort to illuminate the way forward. Every step feels heavy, weighed down by the burden of existential questions and anguish.

In the throes of soul desolation, the things that once brought joy and meaning to life now seem hollow and meaningless. Relationships feel strained, prayers go unanswered, and even the simplest pleasures lose their luster. It's as though a dark cloud has descended upon the soul, casting a shadow over every aspect of existence.

# The Tapestry of Life

Despair becomes a constant companion, whispering lies of worthlessness and hopelessness into the ear of the afflicted soul. The future appears bleak and uncertain, and the past feels like a distant dream — a time when happiness was within reach, but now lies beyond grasp.

Desolation of the soul is not merely a state of sadness or despair; it is a spiritual wilderness where the familiar landmarks of faith seem distant and unreachable. Like the psalmist crying out from the depths of anguish, we may feel abandoned and forgotten by Heaven's corridors. Even the most well-meaning words of encouragement may ring hollow against the deafening silence of inner turmoil.

In the Christian tradition, the journey through soul desolation mirrors the path of Jesus in the wilderness. Just as Jesus faced temptation and struggle, so too do we confront our inner demons and doubts. Yet, it is in the wilderness that Jesus found clarity and strength to fulfill His purpose. Similarly, our soul's desolation can be a crucible for growth and renewal.

During these incredibly difficult sojourns, it's essential to lean into practices of faith and self-care. Prayer, meditation, and seeking solace in Christian community can provide strength and comfort. It's also crucial to acknowledge our feelings without judgment, allowing ourselves to experience the full depth of our emotions.

Moreover, desolation of the spirit invites us to cultivate resilience and trust in the midst of uncertainty. Just as the darkest nights give way to the dawn, so too does our despair pave the way for hope to emerge. It is through this process of surrender, and surrendering, that we discover the transformative power of grace.

As we navigate the wilderness of our souls, let us remember that desolation is not the end of the journey but a sacred invitation to deeper intimacy with the Person of God. May we embrace the darkness as a prelude to the dawn, knowing that even in our darkest moments, we are held in the loving embrace of God's grace.

# The Wounds of Betrayal

In the journey of life, few wounds cut as deeply as the betrayal of trust. Whether it's a friend's deceit, a partner's infidelity, or a colleague's treachery, the pain can feel like a jagged knife carving through your soul. Betrayal shatters the very foundation of trust we build with others, leaving behind a chaotic landscape of emotions that can take years to navigate.

Betrayal is not just a wound; it's a persistent ache that lingers, a shadow that refuses to lift. When someone we trust betrays us, it doesn't just fracture our perception of them—it upends our entire sense of security and faith in humanity. The emotional scars from such a breach run deep, often weaving their way into our daily lives, affecting how we see the world and ourselves.

In the wake of betrayal, a maelstrom of emotions is inevitable—anger, hurt, sadness, confusion. We may find ourselves caught in an endless loop of self-doubt, questioning if we missed the signs or if we were somehow at fault. These feelings are valid, yet they can also become stumbling blocks on the path to healing if we allow them to dominate our thoughts. It's essential to acknowledge these emotions and grant ourselves the grace to feel them, but true healing begins when we make the conscious choice to loosen the grip of bitterness and resentment.

One of the greatest hurdles in the aftermath of betrayal is the daunting task of learning to trust again. The fear of being hurt once more can lead us to erect impenetrable walls around our hearts, isolating ourselves in a fortress of solitude. However, true healing doesn't come from shutting the world out; it comes from daring to open ourselves up to the possibility of trust once more. It's a perilous journey, a leap of faith into the unknown, but it's a necessary step toward growth and restoration.

Acknowledging our pain is essential, but it's equally important to avoid being consumed by it. Healing begins with the conscious decision to let go of bitterness. This does not mean forgetting or excusing the betrayal, but rather refusing to let it define our lives. It's about reclaiming our narrative and moving forward with a heart that, while scarred, remains open to the possibility of trust and love.

Relearning to trust after betrayal is one of the hardest parts of the healing journey. The fear of being hurt again can make us build barriers around our hearts, isolating us from potential connections. But true healing requires us to take risks, to venture out from behind these protective walls. Trusting again is an act of bravery, a testament to our resilience and our belief in the goodness that still exists in the world.

In these dark times, we can find comfort in knowing that we are not alone. There is One who understands our anguish deeply, having experienced the sting of betrayal from those closest to Him. Jesus Christ, betrayed by a disciple and abandoned by His friends, responded with forgiveness and love. His grace offers us a model for how to navigate our pain—through forgiveness, not because the betrayer deserves it, but because we deserve peace.

Forgiveness is not a one-time act but a process. It's a journey we undertake for our own sake, to free ourselves from the chains of resentment. It doesn't mean we must reconcile with those who hurt us, but it does mean we release their hold over our hearts and minds.

Let us hold on to the promise that God heals the brokenhearted and binds up their wounds. In moments of prayer and quiet reflection, we can turn our pain over to Him, trusting that He will guide us toward healing. By surrendering our wounds to His care, we open ourselves to the transformative power of love and grace.

# The Wounds of Betrayal

Though the path is steep and the night dark, the dawn will come. We will find peace again, not in spite of our scars, but because of them. They will be reminders of our strength, our capacity for forgiveness, and the endless depth of God's love for us.

# The Privilege of Old Age

As the sun sets on the landscape of life, casting long shadows across the years, we find ourselves in the sacred season of old age. The body, once resilient and vibrant, now bears the weight of time – a vessel weathered by the journey through the seasons of life. Infirmities, both visible and concealed, become companions in this pilgrimage, reminding us of the fragility inherent in our mortal existence. And fears may haunt us, lingering like distant echoes in the recesses of our souls.

Yet, it is in these twilight years that the beauty of grace unfolds in profound ways. The body may grow frail, and the spirit may wrestle with uncertainties, but in the vulnerability of aging, there is an invitation to lean on the everlasting arms of grace. For it is in weakness that strength is perfected, and in the midst of infirmities, we find that God's divine tenderness sustains us.

The fear of the unknown often haunts the aging heart, whispering doubts about the road ahead. But we do not need to allow fear to take a leading role in our lives. Rather, let faith in our good God be the compass that guides the way. Trust in the promise that even in the winter of life, there is a spring of hope waiting to blossom.

# The Tapestry of Life

Old age is a tapestry woven with threads of wisdom and lessons learned. Every wrinkle tells a story, and each gray hair carries the weight of experience. In embracing the reality of aging, we open ourselves to a deep well of gratitude, recognizing that every day is a gift to be cherished.

Let not the fear of diminishing strength overshadow the strength found in enduring love and persevering faith. In these twilight years, we can find comfort in the arms of a God who understands the ebb and flow of time. His grace is sufficient, covering our fears with the warmth of divine assurance.

The Creator, who shaped our beginnings, accompanies us through the journey's twilight. It is in this sacred space that faith becomes a lantern, illuminating the path obscured by the fears and infirmities of old age. The spiritual fortitude cultivated over a lifetime becomes a beacon, guiding us through the labyrinth of uncertainties. We discover that the sunset of life is but a prelude to a dawn where infirmities and fears dissolve in the light of an everlasting hope.

As we navigate the challenges that come with old age, may we discover the beauty that lies within the wrinkles and the peace that surpasses understanding. For in the tapestry of infirmities and fears, the grace of God weaves a masterpiece of resilience, faith, and enduring love.

# LIGHTS IN THE DARKNESS

In the journey of life, we often find ourselves walking through periods of darkness. These are times when uncertainty, pain, and confusion seem to shroud our path. At some points in our lives, the darkness is particularly acute: the loss of physical ability resulting in dependence on others for care; crushing financial circumstances caused by unexpected medical bills or the loss of a job; the death of a spouse or a child; the infirmities and fears of old age; or the betrayal and/or estrangement by a close friend or mate. For some, it is a life-long battle with depression. Sometimes the darkness can be pervasive, persistent, and oppressive. It seems like the darkness will never end.

Yet, in the midst of such profound despair, there are those who, despite their own journeys through deep, personal darkness, still manage to be light. These individuals, through their vulnerability and reliance on God, show the world that their strength comes from Christ. They continue to fight for joy and refuse to give in to despair. They persevere with kindness, still managing to encourage those around them, reaching beyond their own circumstances to serve others.

These special people possess a light all their own. In Matthew 5:14-16, Jesus says, "You are the light of the world. A town built on a hill cannot be hidden…let your light shine before others, that they may see your good deeds and glorify your Father in heaven." The darkness experienced by these people does not extinguish their light. On the contrary, their life with Christ shines all the brighter in contrast to the darkness.

Being a light in the darkness is not about being perfect or having all the answers; it's about reflecting God's love, hope, and grace to those around us. Just as a single candle can pierce through the deepest darkness, our acts of kindness, encouragement, and compassion can bring warmth and hope to those in need.

Imagine the impact of a single flame in a vast, dark cavern. It flickers, dances, and pushes back the oppressive shadows, offering a glimmer of hope and direction. Similarly, our small acts of love and grace, no matter how insignificant they may seem, can provide profound comfort and guidance to those lost in their own darkness.

So, let us embrace the role of being a light in the darkness. Let us be vessels of God's love, spreading His message of hope even when we face our own trials. We can be like lighthouses on a stormy sea, guiding weary souls safely to shore. Our own struggles can become the very source of our light, showing others that it is possible to find joy amidst suffering.

When we choose to let our light shine, we are not only transforming our own hearts but also Illuminating the lives of others. We remind them that they are not alone in their struggles and that there is a beacon of hope even in the darkest times. We don't have to wait for life to no longer be hard in order to choose joy. By choosing joy in the midst of hardship, we can become a testament to the enduring power of faith and the unending love of God.

# Fighting for Joy

In the tapestry of existence, there are moments when the sheer act of living becomes a battleground, and joy appears to be a distant casualty. Let's face it...sometimes life can be extraordinarily tough. Arduous. Painful. In these times, we must recognize the importance of fighting for joy, not merely existing but truly living.

The fight for joy is intertwined with the fight for life itself. It's a recognition that life's journey is not just about surviving but about thriving, embracing the fullness of each moment. Too often, the weight of challenges can lead us into a state of mere existence, where joy is relegated to a distant dream. However, the fight for joy compels us to break free from the shackles of monotony and reclaim the vibrancy that life offers.

To fight for joy is to cultivate a resilient spirit. Life's battles may leave scars, but within those scars lies evidence of our strength and perseverance. The fight for joy invites us to view challenges not as insurmountable obstacles but as opportunities for growth. It's an acknowledgment that, even in the midst of adversity, joy can be a guiding force, lighting the path towards a more meaningful existence.

Living, not just existing, involves intentional choices. It requires us to purposefully, actively seek out moments of joy, even in the smallest details of life. Whether it's savoring the warmth of sunlight on a chilly day or relishing the laughter of loved ones, the fight for joy prompts us to be present, to engage fully with the richness of our experiences.

Moreover, the fight for joy is a spiritual endeavor. It entails connecting with a deeper sense of purpose and gratitude, recognizing that life's true abundance goes beyond material possessions. Spiritual nourishment provides the sustenance needed to navigate the complexities of existence with grace and resilience.

In the battle for joy, let us not merely exist but live with purpose, passion, and gratitude.

As we embrace the fight for joy, we discover that it is not a selfish pursuit but a transformative journey that radiates grace and purpose, influencing not only our lives, but also the lives of those around us. Through this fight, we unlock the true essence of living—a journey marked by perseverance and illuminated by the radiant glow of joy.

# THE SUFFICIENCY OF GOD

In the tapestry of life, uncertainties often weave their threads, leaving us with frayed edges of doubt and anxiety. In such moments, the concept of God's sufficiency emerges as a beacon of hope, offering security and assurance.

God's sufficiency means that He is more than enough for all our needs. It transcends the limits of human understanding, encompassing every facet of our existence. In times of scarcity, His abundance overflows; in moments of weakness, His strength becomes our foundation.

The Bible resounds with verses that echo the theme of God's sufficiency. One such passage is found in 2 Corinthians 12:9, where God declares, "My grace is sufficient for you, for my power is made perfect in weakness." This profound truth beckons us to relinquish our self-reliance and trust in the boundless sufficiency of God's grace.

As we navigate the complexities of life, it's tempting to seek fulfillment in temporal pursuits, relationships, or accomplishments. However, the psalmist reminds us in Psalm 16:5 that, "Lord, you alone are my portion and my cup; you make my lot secure." The sufficiency of God is not merely a theological concept but a lived reality, shaping our identity, and providing an unshakable foundation.

When we face challenges that seem insurmountable, it is tempting to rely on our own strength, intellect, or resources. Yet, the very essence of God's sufficiency lies in surrendering our inadequacies to Him. In doing so, we open ourselves to the transformative power of His grace, discovering that His strength is perfected in our moments of weakness.

Moreover, God's sufficiency extends beyond material needs to the depths of our emotional and spiritual well-being. In times of sorrow, He offers comfort; in moments of confusion, He provides wisdom. As we navigate the intricate tapestry of life, His sufficiency becomes the anchor that steadies our souls.

Embracing the sufficiency of God is an ongoing journey of trust and dependency. It requires a conscious decision to release our grip on control and embrace the certainty of His provision. In this surrender, we find a profound, transcendent peace—a peace that emanates from the unwavering truth that God is more than enough for every circumstance.

May the realization of God's sufficiency permeate our hearts, transforming our worries into worship and our doubts into deepened faith. In Him, we find completeness, and in His sufficiency, we discover the profound beauty of a life anchored in the unchanging nature of our Creator.

# Living from a Grace-Based Perspective

Living life from a grace-based perspective is an invitation to embrace the profound and unmerited favor of God. Grace is the cornerstone of a life transformed, offering a lens through which we can view our own journey and the world around us.

In a grace-based life, we recognize that our worth is not earned but freely given. It liberates us from the burden of perfectionism and the relentless pursuit of approval. Understanding that we are unconditionally loved, and accepted, by a gracious Creator allows us to extend that grace to ourselves and others. Every step becomes a dance with divine favor, a celebration of being chosen and cherished.

Grace also empowers us to navigate life's challenges with resilience and hope. In moments of failure or hardship, a grace-based perspective reminds us that mistakes do not define us. Instead of dwelling on shortcomings, we can learn, grow, and move forward with a spirit of humility and gratitude for the grace that sustains us.

Living in grace prompts a heart of gratitude. Each day becomes an opportunity to marvel at the unearned blessings that surround us. From the warmth of the sun to the kindness of a friend, grace permeates every aspect of our existence. Gratitude becomes a natural response, creating a positive cycle of appreciation and acknowledgment of the abundant grace we've received.

Furthermore, a grace-based life fosters compassion for others. Recognizing our own need for grace, we approach others with empathy rather than judgment. In moments of conflict or misunderstanding, we extend the same grace we have received, fostering unity, understanding, and reconciliation.

Relationships flourish in the soil of grace. Extending grace to others means choosing understanding over judgment, forgiveness over resentment. It opens the door to empathy, fostering connections built on acceptance rather than unrealistic expectations. A grace-based perspective allows us to appreciate the uniqueness of individuals, understanding that everyone is on a journey.

Ultimately, living life from a grace-based perspective transforms our worldview. It shifts our focus from performance to purpose, from fear to freedom. As we walk in the light of grace, our lives become a testament to the unmerited favor that sustains and propels us forward. May our days be marked by grace—grace received, grace given, and grace lived out in every interaction and circumstance.

# THE SACRED ACT OF LISTENING

There is very little within the realm of human connection that is more highly treasured than attentive presence. To have a person silence the distractions of the outside world, and solely focus on the inner world of the soul of another, is a sacred act of love. Paul Tillich's words captures the essence of a ministry of presence when he said, "the first duty of love is to listen."(Tillich, Paul. *The Art of Being*. New York: Random House, 1962.) [KS12] This poignant reminder invites us to transcend the superficial layers of love, urging us to delve into the holy place of attentive listening.

Love, often depicted through grand gestures and eloquent expressions, finds its most potent manifestation in the subtle cadence of listening. In a world abuzz with incessant noise, where voices clamor for attention, Tillich's words beckon us to cultivate the art of profound receptivity. To truly love is to create a sanctuary for the narratives of others, allowing their unspoken depths to unfold in the hallowed space of our undivided attention.

In the realm of relationships, be they familial, platonic, or romantic, listening becomes the sacred bridge that spans the chasm of understanding. It is a healing communion where empathy and compassion find their roots, where the silent language of the heart is fluently spoken. Through attentive ears, we weave a tapestry of connection, stitching together the threads of shared vulnerability and mutual understanding.

Tillich's insight extends beyond the bounds of personal relationships, resonating with the broader tapestry of humanity. In the tumult of societal discord, the first duty of love is to listen, not merely to the harmonies that echo our own sentiments, but to the dissonant chords that reveal the diverse symphony of perspectives. True love, in this context, becomes a force that dismantles barriers and builds bridges, fostering a collective harmony that transcends individual echoes.

In the quietude of listening, we discover the sacred dance of love—the dance that whispers affirmation to the soul, that validates the existence of the other, and that, in its purest form, binds us all in a symphony of shared humanity. Tillich's wisdom invites us to partake in this dance, to embrace the transformative power of attentive love, and in doing so, to contribute to the harmonious melody of our shared existence together.

# The Simplest Form of Gratitude

Karl Barth wrote, "Joy is the simplest form of gratitude." (Barth, Karl. *The Epistle to the Romans*. Translated by Edwyn C. Hoskyns. London: Oxford University Press, 1933.) [KS13] In contemplating Barth's words, we are invited into a reflection on the essence of gratitude. Barth encapsulates a profound truth – that joy, in its purest and simplest form, is the natural expression of a grateful heart.

Gratitude finds its most genuine manifestation in joy. In the tapestry of human emotions, joy emerges as the thread woven seamlessly with gratitude. It is an acknowledgment, an appreciation that transcends words, finding its voice in the radiant glow of joy.

True joy is not contingent on circumstances but is rooted in a grateful perspective. We recognize the myriad blessings that populate our lives – the small victories, the whispered moments of grace, and the interconnected threads that make up the fabric of our existence. Joy becomes the melody that arises when we pause to appreciate the symphony of life.

Joy, like a radiant sunbeam, emanates from the core of our being when we recognize and cherish the blessings bestowed upon us. It is not merely a fleeting emotion but a visceral acknowledgment of the goodness that graces our existence. In its simplicity, joy becomes a pure expression of gratitude, a heart's response to the beauty and grace that surround us.

# The Tapestry of Life

To experience joy is to engage in a dance with gratitude, a dance that transcends the complexities of life. It is an acknowledgment that goes beyond words, reaching into the depths of our souls. In moments of joy, we find ourselves immersed in a profound sense of thankfulness, appreciating the tapestry of life woven with threads of both challenge and triumph.

Gratitude, in its purest form, is often found in the simplicity of joyous moments—a shared laughter, a gentle breeze, or the warmth of a loving embrace. When joy becomes the lens through which we view the world, gratitude becomes a natural response, an attitude that transforms our perspective on life's journey.

In the simplicity of joy, we discover the richness of gratitude. It is a spiritual practice that transcends circumstances, reminding us that even in the midst of trials, there is always something to be thankful for. Karl Barth's words echo a profound truth: joy, with its radiant simplicity, is indeed the purest and simplest form of gratitude—a testament to the interconnectedness of our hearts with the abundant gifts life presents to us.

# A Grace-Led Life

In the intricate tapestry of existence, the threads of grace are woven with divine artistry, creating a narrative that transcends our flaws and shortcomings. Each thread of grace is a reminder of the unfathomable love and mercy that guide us through the twists and turns of our earthly pilgrimage.

Grace is not a distant concept but a tangible gift, freely bestowed upon us. It beckons us to embrace imperfection with humility, reminding us in moments of weakness that we are not defined by our mistakes but by the boundless compassion extended to us by God. Each step taken in the light of grace is a step towards redemption, a testament to the transformative power of unconditional love lavished upon us by our Creator.

Living a grace-led life involves extending that same grace to others. It's a recognition that everyone carries their burdens and stumbles along their path. Compassion becomes the currency of interaction, understanding that we are all flawed travelers seeking solace in our shared humanity. In the mirror of grace, judgment dissipates, making room for empathy and connection.

Grace empowers us to break free from the shackles of guilt and shame, offering a chance for renewal. It is a relentless tide, washing away the debris of past mistakes, leaving behind a shoreline of second chances. In the face of adversity, a grace-led life stands resilient, anchored in the belief that even the darkest storms can be weathered with the unwavering assurance of divine support.

## The Tapestry of Life

As we navigate the intricacies of life's tapestry, let grace be the thread that binds us to the sacred rhythm of existence. In moments of triumph, let gratitude be our melody, and in moments of challenge, let grace be our anchor. For it is through grace that we discover the profound beauty of a life led by love, forgiveness, and the boundless mercy that transcends our understanding.

# Committing No Errors and Still Losing

In the tapestry of our lives, the threads are often woven with precision and care. We strive for excellence, meticulously avoiding mistakes, holding fast to the belief that our diligence will yield the fruit of success. Yet, in the quiet of our hearts, we know a sobering truth: it is possible to commit no errors and still lose.

This paradoxical reality can leave us feeling bewildered and disheartened. We might think of the athlete who trains tirelessly, executing every movement flawlessly, yet fails to stand atop the podium. We remember the student who studies diligently, mastering the material, only to find the examination asks questions they did not foresee. Or the diligent worker, whose every effort and innovation is unrecognized, as the company shutters its doors.

The weight of such experiences can be crushing, leaving us questioning the very fabric of our efforts and the worth of our striving. How can it be, we wonder, that despite our unwavering commitment and near-perfection, the outcome slips through our fingers like sand?

Scripture offers us a glimpse into this perplexing truth through the life of Job. Here was a man of impeccable character, blameless and upright, who feared God and shunned evil. Despite his unwavering fidelity and righteousness, Job experienced profound loss and suffering. His livestock, servants, and children were taken from him in a series of tragic events. He sat in ashes, covered in sores, bewildered by the calamity that had befallen him despite his faithfulness.

In Job's story, we see the raw reality of human suffering and the inexplicable nature of some of our losses. It is a stark reminder that righteousness does not guarantee a life free from pain or disappointment. Job's friends, convinced that suffering must be the result of sin or error, urged him to repent for wrongdoing he had not committed. But the book of Job reveals a deeper truth: our struggles are not always a reflection of our failures.

In the face of loss, we may find ourselves grappling with doubt and despair. The emptiness of our unfulfilled expectations can seem like a chasm too vast to bridge. Yet, it is in these moments of profound vulnerability that we can encounter the sustaining presence of God.

The apostle Paul, writing to the Corinthians, reminds us that our labor is not in vain. "Therefore, my beloved brethren, be steadfast, immovable, always abounding in the work of the Lord, knowing that your toil is not in vain in the Lord" (1 Corinthians 15:58). This assurance does not promise us earthly success, but it does offer a divine perspective: our efforts, aligned with God's purposes, have eternal significance beyond our immediate outcomes.

As we navigate the complexities of our journey, let us find comfort in the truth that God's measure of success transcends our finite understanding. When we commit no errors and still lose, it does not diminish our worth or the value of our efforts. Our faithfulness, our perseverance in the face of adversity, are precious in the eyes of God.

In the quiet aftermath of our losses, let us draw near to the One who knows our every tear and heartache. Let us rest in His unfailing love, trusting that even when the world does not applaud our endeavors, we are held by the One whose love and grace are boundless. Though we may not always see the fruits of our labor in this life, we can be assured that in God's economy, nothing is wasted. Our struggles, our strivings, and our seemingly lost battles, all find their place in His grand tapestry, woven with threads of hope, purpose, and divine love.

# The Miracle of a Moment

In the hustle and busyness of our daily lives, we often overlook the profound beauty concealed within the simplicity of a moment. Every breath we take, every beat of our heart, is a testament to the miracle of life. Each moment is a divine gift, a sacred opportunity to experience the richness of existence. Recognize the hand of God as He intricately crafts the tapestry of our lives.

Consider the sunrise, a celestial spectacle that graces the sky with radiant hues of warmth and hope. In that fleeting moment, there is a miraculous transformation, a reminder that darkness cannot withstand the power of light. Life, too, is a series of sunrises—moments of renewal, grace, and the promise of a new beginning. As the first light of dawn pierces the horizon, it heralds the start of a new day, filled with endless possibilities. It is in this daily rebirth that we are invited to witness the grandeur of God's creation, to marvel at the brilliance of His artistry.

The miracle of a moment lies not only in its beauty but in its impermanence. Just as a sunset bids farewell to the day, moments pass, making room for the next. This transience compels us to cherish each instant, for once it slips away, it becomes a memory. Yet, in the realm of memory, the miracle endures—a timeless echo of joy, love, or even hardship overcome. Memories are the silent storytellers of our lives, whispering tales of laughter, tears, and growth. They remind us that each fleeting moment is a chapter in the grand narrative of our existence, each one significant in its own right.

# The Tapestry of Life

Think about the laughter shared with loved ones around a table, the warmth of a hug, or the tranquility found in a quiet moment of reflection. These seemingly ordinary instances harbor extraordinary depth when we recognize them as threads woven into the fabric of our journey. The sound of laughter, a hug's gentle embrace, or a peaceful moment of solitude can be profound reminders of our interconnectedness and the love that binds us. These are the moments that define us, that shape our character and our faith.

The fabric of life is composed of a myriad of moments; some glittering with joy and others draped in the shadows of challenges. In our pursuit of grand milestones, we may neglect the miracles woven into the fabric of our everyday lives. The mundane becomes sacred when we pause to appreciate it. Each moment is a brushstroke in the masterpiece of our existence, contributing to the larger narrative of our journey. Every seemingly insignificant detail adds texture and color to the grand canvas of our lives, transforming it into a work of art.

As we navigate the wonder of time, let us not overlook the significance of the present. The miracle of a moment is not confined to grand events but is found in the simplicity of a shared smile, the gentle breeze on our face, or the quiet realization that we are alive. Embrace these miracles, for in doing so, we unlock the profound depth of a life well-lived—one moment at a time. To truly live is to appreciate each breath, to savor each experience, and to find joy in the ordinary. It is in the present moment that we find the essence of life, the heartbeat of our existence, and the whisper of God's love.

# Relinquishing the Right to be Right

In the quiet corners of our hearts, there lies a relentless urge—to be right. It's a whisper that becomes a roar in the heat of conflict, a need that pulses with every disagreement. But what if we could silence that roar, and in its place, hear the gentle call of peace and humility?

Jesus, our greatest example, embodied this radical humility. Though He was God incarnate, He did not cling to His divine privileges. Philippians 2:6-7 reminds us, "Who, being in very nature God, did not consider equality with God something to be used to his own advantage; rather, he made himself nothing by taking the very nature of a servant, being made in human likeness." Imagine the magnitude of this humility: the Creator of the universe, choosing to serve rather than to dominate, to love rather than to demand reverence.

When we insist on being right, it often stems from a deep-rooted fear—fear of being misunderstood, fear of losing control, fear of feeling insignificant. These fears can chain us to a cycle of conflict and self-righteousness. Yet, in relinquishing the right to be right, we break these chains, and step into the liberating grace of God.

Consider the pain of an argument with a loved one. Words are sharp, tempers flare, and before we know it, the rift widens. In those heated moments, what we crave most is not to be right but to be heard, to be understood, and to be valued. James 1:19-20 gently guides us: "Everyone should be quick to listen, slow to speak and slow to become angry, because human anger does not produce the righteousness that God desires." Imagine the transformative power of these words if we lived them out—listening with the intent to understand, speaking with kindness, and letting go of anger.

There is profound strength in choosing humility over pride. Abraham exemplified this when he allowed Lot to choose the best land, even though he had every right to claim it. Genesis 13 shows us a man who valued peace and relationship over asserting his rights. This act of humility didn't diminish Abraham; instead, it magnified God's blessings in his life.

The apostle Paul, in Colossians 3:12-15, paints a beautiful picture of the virtues that should clothe our hearts: "Compassion, kindness, humility, gentleness, and patience… And over all these virtues put on love, which binds them all together in perfect unity." These are not mere words; they are a call to transform our very nature, to let love bind us in perfect unity. When we choose these virtues, we reflect the very heart of Christ.

Relinquishing the right to be right is a crucible—it burns away the dross of pride and leaves the pure gold of love and humility. It's a daily surrender, a moment-by-moment choice to echo Jesus' prayer, "Not my will, but Yours be done." It's in this surrender that we find true peace, not only within our hearts but also in our relationships.

Imagine the ripple effect of such a choice: a home filled with understanding, a community woven with threads of kindness, or a world where love triumphs over division. This is the kingdom of God made manifest in our midst.

Let us pray for the strength to embrace this path of humility. May we be quick to listen, slow to speak, and eager to love. In relinquishing our right to be right, we gain so much more—peace, unity, and a deeper reflection of Christ's love in our lives. May His grace empower us to live out this calling every day.

# Trusting God in Difficulty

Life is an unspeakably precious gift we have the privilege of enjoying each day. Every day. With the rising of the sun, we rise... to experience a brand-new gift of twenty-four unblemished hours, full of possibilities and potential.[KS15]

Many of us have had a brush with our own mortality. Whether it be a very serious health problem, a near-miss traffic accident, or a work-related accident...some of us have come right up to the very precipice of our existence and have been able to walk back from death's grasp. Often times, those experiences result in physical limitations/debilitation or emotional scars that will be with us for the rest of our lives here on planet Earth. But they are reminders of what could have happened, mentors that teach us to treasure every moment, every breath.

Coming face to face with our own mortality drives home how good, and how precious life is. Such experiences bring forth great gratitude for the joy of one more day with our spouses, one more day with our families, one more day of companionship with our friends and co-workers, one more day to make a difference, one more day to relish life on God's good Earth, one more day to forgive and be forgiven, and one more day to experience and extend grace.

Life is a priceless gift beyond words, a treasure we're granted anew each dawn. With the sun's ascent, we rise to embrace twenty-four pristine hours, brimming with promise and opportunity.

# The Tapestry of Life

Many of us have glimpsed our own mortality. Whether through severe illness, a close call on the road, or a workplace incident, some have stood at the edge of existence and stepped back from death's grasp. These encounters often leave us with lasting physical or emotional wounds, etched reminders of what might have been—a constant nudge to cherish every moment, every breath.

Confronting mortality underscores life's profound goodness and preciousness. It ignites deep gratitude for each extra day with loved ones, for the companionship of friends and colleagues, for the chance to make a meaningful impact. Each day becomes a gift: to savor the beauty of God's creation, to extend forgiveness and receive it, and to embrace and share grace in abundance.

Even our hardships remind us we are alive; we are still here. If life is hard, it means you still possess the treasure of life. We do not need to wait for the hardships to end in order to be joy-filled, to experience happiness and contentment. Joy is a choice, as is gratitude.

Difficulty brings clarity and helps us appreciate our lives in ways we did not prior to adversity. We may even grow to the point where we become grateful for suffering pain and adversity, for it helps us to be grateful that we are alive for one more day.

This is a game-changing paradigm shift in how we approach our days. But watch what happens to you, and to those around you, as you walk as a thankful person. Gratitude is perhaps the key characteristic whereby a genuine child of God is recognized.

Trust God's authorship of your life and how He brings each day into being. When was the last time you expressed unbridled, unconditional gratitude to God for life? For the joy of just being alive? For the tremendous blessings we enjoy each day?

Live in gratitude today. Choose joy. Be kind and compassionate. Make no demands of God or others. Just enjoy being. Thank God throughout your day for life.

# The Battle for Joy

In life's chaotic symphony, joy often feels like a distant melody, drowned out by the cacophony of challenges and uncertainties. The enemy seeks to steal our joy, whispering doubts and casting shadows over our hearts. Days may go by— even weeks— with little or no relief from the relentless grind of unyielding demands, the desperate emptiness of the soul, and the crushing weight of despondency and despair. Happiness seems like a hollow, distant echo of days far removed from us, a memory that mocks our present suffering.

Yet, in the heat of this battle, we are reminded of our strength— that joy isn't a passive state but a deliberate choice. It's choosing to bloom amidst the cracks, to find light in the darkest tunnels, and to embrace hope when despair attempts to reign. Joy is an act of rebellion against the forces that seek to pull us into the abyss.

Scripture reminds us that joy isn't circumstantial but a gift from God, transcending our situations. It's a choice, a deliberate stance against despair, forged in the crucible of adversity. Joy isn't the absence of difficulties but the steadfast confidence in God's sovereignty amidst them. It's the assurance that, even in our darkest hours, we are held by a love that is unshakeable and eternal.

To fight for joy, we must cultivate a grateful heart. Gratitude unlocks the door to joy, helping us discover beauty amid ashes, and finding comfort in the smallest blessings. It's in the simple moments—a child's laughter, a sunset's glow, and a friend's comforting words—where we find glimpses of God's grace. Gratitude shifts our focus from scarcity to abundance, from despair to hope, and from pain to healing. It transforms our vision, allowing us to see the hand of God in every detail of our lives, no matter how small.

Another weapon in our arsenal is to shift our perspective from the immediate to the eternal. When storms rage, we can fix our gaze on the horizon beyond the tempest. Our present troubles, though daunting, are temporary, while the joy set before us is eternal. This eternal perspective empowers us to endure with hopeful anticipation, knowing that the struggles we face now are but a fleeting moment in the grand tapestry of God's plan.

To fight for joy is to wield gratitude as a shield against negativity, to find shelter in the beauty of small victories, and to nurture a heart that seeks joy despite the adversity we face. It's a choice to rise, to dust off the ashes of defeat, and to embrace joy as an act of defiance against despair. It's the courage to believe that, even in our brokenness, we are being made whole.

Lastly, community plays a vital role. Sharing our burdens and joys with others not only lightens our load but also fosters empathy, encouragement, and shared celebrations. Together, we bolster each other's spirits in the pursuit of joy. In the fellowship of believers, we find strength and solace, reminding each other of the joy that is ours in Christ.

Fighting for joy isn't passive; it's an intentional, ongoing battle. By equipping ourselves with gratitude, perspective, surrender, and community, we can persevere through life's trials, knowing that joy, a fruit of the Spirit, is within our grasp. The Christian experience is not for wimps. It requires us to be tough-minded, soft-hearted children of the Living God. Therefore, take heart, for in this battle for joy, we are not alone. God stands with us, offering strength, grace, and the promise of an enduring, abundant joy that surpasses all understanding.

In the end, joy is not a distant dream but a present reality we can grasp. It is a beacon of hope in a world often shrouded in darkness, a light that never dims because its source is the eternal, unchanging love of God. So, fight for your joy with all your might, knowing that this battle is one worth waging, and that victory is already ours in Christ.

# WILLING THE WILL OF GOD AFTER HIM

The Dean of the seminary I attended, Dr. James Grier, said that the greatest good a Christian could do in this world was to "will the will of God after Him with ever-increasing spontaneity and joy." On the surface, these words may sound cold and academic, but in reality, they encapsulate the heart of what it means to grow as a child of God, a heart bursting with the warmth and vibrancy of divine purpose.

"Willing the will of God after Him with increasing spontaneity and joy" is more than just a lofty ideal; it is an invitation to embrace a profound spiritual alignment, a sacred journey where our deepest desires and intentions become harmonious with God's perfect plans for our lives. This journey begins with a heartfelt surrender—a surrender not born of weakness or resignation but of trust and reverence, an act of profound faith in the wisdom and love of our Creator.

When we choose to yield our will to God's, we enter into a dynamic partnership with Him, one where we discover a peace that surpasses all understanding. This peace is not the absence of trials but the presence of God amid them, a steady assurance that His plans are far greater than our own. As we walk this path, we learn that willing God's will is not a rigid, joyless submission but a vibrant, life-giving alignment. It's a continuous unfolding of our hearts, attuned to His, seeking alignment in every facet of our existence. This alignment invites a spontaneous response to His calling, a readiness to act in accordance with His divine guidance with an open heart and willing spirit.

The joy that comes from this alignment signifies a profound transformation within us. It is a deep-seated contentment in knowing that God's will is not a set of restrictive rules but a pathway to true liberation. Embracing His purpose for our lives brings a fulfillment that transcends the fleeting happiness of this world, nurturing a sustained and deeper joy rooted in our spiritual connection with Him.

Yet, this journey is not without its challenges. There are times when our own desires clash with what we perceive as God's will, moments of tension and struggle. But even in these moments, there is opportunity for growth. We learn to seek clarity, wisdom, and discernment through His word, through prayer, and through reflective communion with Him. We trust that God's plan, though sometimes mysterious, unfolds in perfect timing, leading us to places of greater understanding and peace.

The increasing spontaneity in embracing His will comes from a growing intimacy with God. As our relationship with Him deepens, we develop a profound trust that enables us to respond spontaneously to His nudges and whispers. We come to know with certainty that His guidance is always rooted in love and infinite wisdom.

In the end, "willing the will of God after Him with increasing spontaneity and joy" is a transformative journey—a journey of finding harmony, joy, and purpose in divine alignment. It is allowing His will to become the heartbeat of our existence, guiding our steps with ever-increasing spontaneity, and filling our hearts with unending joy.

May our hearts be open to His guidance, our spirits receptive to His leading, and our lives a testament to the immeasurable joy found in surrendering to His perfect will. Let us embrace this journey with trust and joy, knowing that in willing His will, we are participating in the greatest good we can do in this world.

# "I'm Too Busy"

In the relentless rush of life, it's all too easy to find ourselves ensnared in the suffocating grip of perpetual busyness. The phrase "I'm too busy" becomes a familiar refrain, a convenient shield against further commitments, and a justification for neglecting the things that truly matter. Yet, amidst this chaotic whirlwind, lies a profound opportunity for reflection and growth.

Busyness in itself isn't inherently negative; it's our approach to prioritizing time that truly shapes our lives. Often, our hectic schedules are born from the choices we make—the tasks we deem urgent, the pursuits we prioritize, and the obligations we commit to. It's crucial, in the throes of these demands, to remember the significance of balance and intentional living.

Consider the life of Jesus, who faced ceaseless demands on His time. Despite this, He intentionally made space for what truly mattered—time with His Father, moments of solitude, and meaningful interactions with others. He didn't allow the tyranny of busyness to dictate His life; rather, He lived with purpose and intentionality, drawing strength, guidance, and renewal from His time spent in quiet reflection and communion. This enabled Him to carry out His mission with unwavering resolve and profound compassion.

When we habitually claim to be too busy, we might be missing out on precious opportunities to nurture relationships, pursue our passions, or even care for our own well-being. This is a poignant moment to reevaluate our priorities and ask ourselves if our busyness aligns with our core values. It calls for discerning between what is truly important and what is merely urgent, understanding that the two are not always the same.

Rather than using "I'm too busy" as an excuse, let's embrace it as an invitation for deep reflection. Take a step back, reassess commitments, and create space for the things that bring joy, fulfillment, and spiritual nourishment. Embrace mindfulness and intentional scheduling. Have the courage to say no to activities and demands that don't align with your true purpose.

It's not about having an empty schedule, but rather a purposeful one. Cultivate a rhythm that allows for rest, growth, and meaningful connection—both with others and with your deeper spiritual self. Let go of the glorification of busyness and embrace a life guided by intention, balance, and the pursuit of what truly matters.

In a world that prizes productivity and haste, let's dare to prioritize differently. Imagine a life where our schedules reflect our deepest values, where we find time for the quiet whisper of God's voice amidst the clamor of our daily routines. Picture the richness of relationships that flourish because we have chosen to invest time in them. Envision a life where our daily activities are not just filled with tasks but are infused with purpose and meaning.

As we navigate the demands of our days, let us draw inspiration from Jesus' example. May we seek out moments of solitude to reconnect with our spiritual center, moments of genuine connection with those we love, and moments of purposeful action that align with our deepest values. In doing so, we'll find that the chaos of busyness can be transformed into a symphony of intentional living, where each note is played with purpose, passion, and a deep sense of fulfillment.

# THE ART OF BEING

In a world that constantly demands more from us—more productivity, more engagement, and more achievement—it's easy to lose sight of the simple yet profound importance of just being. We are bombarded with messages that equate our worth with our accomplishments, leaving us perpetually striving, and rarely resting. But in the stillness, in the quiet moments where we let go of doing, and embrace being, we discover a peace that transcends understanding.

Imagine standing at the edge of the ocean, the vast expanse of water stretching endlessly before you. The rhythmic sound of waves crashing against the shore, the salty breeze caressing your skin, and the golden hues of the setting sun painting the sky, create a symphony of tranquility. Here, in this sacred space, time seems to pause, and you are invited to simply be. No demands, no expectations—just the pure, unfiltered experience of existence. Your soul breathes deeply, savoring the beauty of simply being alive. This is the essence of just being.

Jesus often withdrew to solitary places, seeking communion with the Father in stillness and quiet. In Mark 1:35, we read, "Very early in the morning, while it was still dark, Jesus got up, left the house and went off to a solitary place, where he prayed." Jesus understood the necessity of stepping away from the demands of life to be replenished in the presence of God. In these moments of solitude, we too can find rest for our souls, reconnecting with our Creator, and remembering who we truly are.

In our culture, busyness is often celebrated, and rest can feel like a guilty indulgence. Yet, the psalmist reminds us, "Be still, and know that I am God" (Psalm 46:10). This invitation to stillness is a call to trust, to release our grip on control and surrender to the gentle rhythm of God's grace. It is in this surrender that we find the deep, abiding peace our hearts long for.

Consider the ocean, how it ebbs and flows with the tides, ever constant, ever changing. The ocean does not strive or struggle; it simply is a majestic testament to the Creator's care and provision. In the same way, our worth is not dependent on our efforts but on the unchanging love of God. When we cease our striving and rest in His presence, we begin to see ourselves as He sees us—beloved, cherished, and enough.

The practice of just being requires intentionality. It calls us to slow down, to create space for quiet and reflection amidst the clamor of daily life. It might look like a few moments of silence in the morning, a walk along the shoreline, or a simple pause to breathe deeply and remember that we are held by grace. These small acts of presence can transform our hearts, grounding us in the truth of God's love, and anchoring us in His peace.

In the stillness, we hear the whispers of God's Spirit, reminding us that we are not defined by what we do but by who we are—His children. This truth liberates us from the tyranny of busyness and performance, inviting us into a life of rest and trust. As we embrace the importance of just being, we find that we are more attuned to God's presence, more aware of His guidance, and more receptive to His love.

Let us, therefore, cultivate the art of being—of resting in God's presence and allowing His peace to fill our hearts. In the quiet, we find our true selves, beloved and secure in His love. And from this place of deep rest, we are empowered to live with greater clarity, compassion, and purpose. Just being is not a passive state but an active embrace of the life God has given us, a life rooted in His unending love and grace.

# LIVING AS A FORGIVEN PERSON

Forgiveness is a gift we receive and a mantle we wear. It is not merely an act but a state of being that profoundly transforms our hearts and minds. When we embrace forgiveness, we don a cloak of liberation, shedding the burdens of anger and resentment. It's the key that unlocks the door to a life unshackled by the weight of bitterness and grudges, allowing us to walk freely and lightly through the world.

To live as a forgiven person is to understand the magnitude of grace extended to us. Just as we have received forgiveness, we are called to extend it to others, regardless of the depth of their transgressions against us. This calling is not always easy; our humanness may grapple with deep-seated pain, betrayal, or injustice. Yet, in letting go, we find ourselves released from the chains that bind our hearts, experiencing a profound sense of peace and liberation.

Living as a forgiven person means embracing a new narrative. It's a story where our mistakes, flaws, and past failures no longer define us. Instead, it becomes a story of redemption and restoration—a narrative where grace triumphs over guilt and love conquers bitterness. This transformation is not instantaneous but a gradual unfolding of a new identity, one where we see ourselves and others through the lens of compassion and mercy.

Forgiveness grants us the freedom to rewrite our future. It empowers us to break free from the destructive cycle of hurt and retaliation. This freedom does not negate the reality of our pain but allows us to navigate it with a heart unburdened by anger and a spirit open to healing. It is a profound shift from being prisoners of our past to becoming architects of our future, shaping a life marked by grace and peace.

Moreover, living in forgiveness fosters a deep sense of humility. It's a recognition of our own need for grace and an acknowledgment that we, too, stand in constant need of pardon. As we extend forgiveness, we emulate the profound love shown to us, realizing that every act of mercy we offer is a reflection of the mercy we have received. This humility softens our hearts, making us more compassionate and understanding toward others' flaws and failings.

Ultimately, living as a forgiven person involves a spirit of gratitude. Gratitude for the second chances we've been given, for the opportunity to mend broken relationships, and for the chance to grow beyond our past mistakes. This gratitude infuses our lives with a sense of wonder and appreciation, allowing us to see the beauty in each new day and the possibilities it holds.

Let us embrace forgiveness not just as an isolated act but as a lifestyle, a continual practice that shapes our character and our relationships. In doing so, we find a freedom that elevates our spirits, transforms our interactions with others, and allows us to experience the profound joy of living in grace. This journey of forgiveness is not always straightforward, but it is a path worth walking, leading us toward a life filled with peace and joy.

May we walk each day in the lightness of being forgiven, extending that same grace to others, and reveling in the beauty of a life liberated by forgiveness. As we do, we will find that forgiveness is not only a gift we receive but a gift we give, a gift that has the power to transform our lives and the lives of those around us.

# Sweet Dreams

For some of us, the harsh realities of our waking world can, and often do, impose themselves on our sleeping minds. In the quiet hours of the night, our minds often wander into the realm of dreams—a sanctum where thoughts paint vivid landscapes and scenarios. It's within this ethereal canvas that the peace of God can graciously reign, offering a safe harbor and guidance for our souls which have been bruised and battered through the day.

Dreams, often an uncharted territory, can mirror our subconscious fears, worries, and desires. Yet, they can also become a conduit for God's peace to envelop us. The Bible reminds us that God grants sleep to His beloved (Psalm 127:2), allowing us to rest in His care, even as we slumber. The peace of God surpasses human understanding, transcending the boundaries of wakefulness, and seeping into the deepest recesses of our minds. When we invite His peace into our dreams, we open ourselves to a divine tranquility that calms storms within us, bringing clarity to the tangled threads of our thoughts.

Imagine dreams not just as random occurrences but as potential avenues where God's peace can take center stage, reigning over the chaos that may lurk in our subconscious. Our dreams can be transformed into sanctuaries where we experience His calming presence. Picture this: as you drift into sleep, your mind begins to weave the tapestry of a dream. Instead of being filled with the anxieties and uncertainties of the day, it is suffused with a gentle, serene light. This light represents the peace of God, spreading warmth and comfort to every corner of your mind, transforming turbulent waters into a sea of glass.

To invite God's peace into our dreams, we can start with prayerful intent before sleep. Surrendering our worries, fears, and uncertainties to God, we open space for His peace to take precedence in our dreaming minds. Reading and meditating on scriptures about peace and trust can also set the stage for a restful and peaceful night. Visualize yourself placing each worry, like a stone, into God's hands, feeling the weight lift from your shoulders. With each act of surrender, you create room for His peace to fill you, ensuring that when you close your eyes, your mind is a fertile ground for His tranquil touch.

In a world characterized by chaos and uncertainties, the gentle touch of God's peace in our dreams becomes a sanctuary. It's an embrace that whispers reassurance amid the turmoil, instilling a sense of calm that transcends the surreal narratives our minds weave during slumber. Envision your dreams as a vast, open field bathed in golden light, where you can wander freely, unburdened by the constraints of the day. Here, God's peace is like a gentle breeze, softly caressing your spirit, and reminding you that you are safe, cherished, and held.

As we embrace the truth that God's peace can rule even in our dreams, we find comfort in knowing that His presence is not confined by time or consciousness. Whether awake or asleep, we are enveloped in His boundless love and protection. Imagine waking up each morning, not groggy and overwhelmed, but refreshed and invigorated by the night's encounter with divine peace. Your dreams, once a place of restlessness, become a source of strength and serenity.

May we welcome His peace into the depths of our sleep, awakening refreshed by His boundless grace and assurance. Let us trust that as we close our eyes each night, we are not just surrendering to rest but entering a sacred space where God's peace can transform us, heal us, and prepare us to face the new day with renewed hope and courage.

# Forgive Again

Forgiveness. It's a word heavy with meaning, layered with emotions that can be both raw and tender. For some, it brings a sense of release and freedom; for others, it stirs up unresolved pain and resentment. The idea of forgiving, especially when the wounds run deep and the scars are visible, feels like an almost insurmountable challenge. Yet, here we stand, faced with the divine call to forgive not just once, but every time the memory resurfaces.

Every time you remember, forgive again. It's a radical invitation to embark on a journey of profound healing and transformation.

Imagine a moment when a painful memory unexpectedly invades your mind. Your heart tightens, and the familiar sting of hurt resurfaces. It's in this moment, with the rawness of the past pressing heavily on your soul, that you are called to forgive again. Forgiveness is not a single act but a continuous choice, a daily commitment to release the grip of bitterness and anger that can so easily entrap your heart.

Forgiveness is not about forgetting the offense or minimizing the hurt. It's about making a conscious decision to let go of the resentment that threatens to poison your spirit. It's about freeing yourself from the chains of bitterness that keep you tied to the past, unable to fully embrace the present. Each time the memory reappears, it's a chance to reaffirm your commitment to forgiveness, to reclaim your peace, and to restore your emotional well-being.

Think of your heart as a delicate, cherished space. To keep this space serene and welcoming, you must continually clear away the debris of anger and hurt. Unforgiveness is like toxic clutter, suffocating the life and joy that are meant to dwell within you. Every time you remember the offense, it's an opportunity to clear away a little more of that clutter, to forgive again, and to nurture the healing process within your heart.

Jesus, our ultimate example of forgiveness, demonstrated the profound power of forgiving without limits. As He hung on the cross, bearing the weight of humanity's sins, He prayed, "Father, forgive them, for they do not know what they are doing" (Luke 23:34). In His darkest, most excruciating moment, He chose forgiveness. His love was so deep, so boundless, that even in the face of unimaginable suffering, He forgave. Each time we remember the hurt inflicted upon us, we are reminded of His limitless grace and mercy.

Forgiveness is an ongoing journey of letting go. It's about surrendering our right to hold on to anger and choosing instead to embrace grace. It's not easy, and there will be days when the memories flood back with an intensity that feels overwhelming. But in those moments, remember that you are not alone. God's Spirit is with you, empowering you to forgive, helping you release the hurt, and filling you with His peace.

As you continue to walk this path of forgiveness, you'll find that your heart grows lighter, your spirit freer. The memories may still come, but they will no longer have the power to control you. Each act of forgiveness builds a resilience within you, creating a deep reservoir of grace that will overflow into every aspect of your life.

So, when the memories arise and the pain resurfaces, choose to forgive again. Let God's love and grace wash over you, healing the wounds, and restoring your peace. In the continuous act of forgiving, you will discover the beauty of a heart unburdened, a soul liberated, and a life transformed by the relentless power of forgiveness.

# Seasons of Darkness

God is at work amidst the darkness. In the darkest of nights, when uncertainty clouds our vision and shadows loom large, it's easy to feel abandoned or lost. The weight of the unknown can press heavily on our hearts, making every step feel like a struggle. Yet, it's precisely in these moments, when all seems bleak and hopeless, that God's handiwork often becomes most evident. His presence, though sometimes imperceptible, is woven through the fabric of our trials, guiding us with a light that pierces even the deepest shadows.

Scripture reminds us time and again that even in the depths of darkness, God is at work, orchestrating His plans for our lives. As the star of Bethlehem pierced the darkness of a bleak world's night sky 2,000 years ago, so too does the light of Christ dispel the deepest shadows of our soul. This divine light brings clarity where confusion reigns and peace where turmoil thrives.

In the book of Genesis, we see how God worked in the darkness of chaos, bringing forth light and creation. The world, once a formless void, was transformed by His command into a masterpiece of order and beauty. Similarly, in our lives, when situations seem bleak and hopeless, God is at work, preparing something beautiful. Just as a seed germinates and takes root in the darkness of the soil before blossoming into a magnificent flower, our growth often begins in the shadows of adversity. These hidden moments of struggle and pain are where God cultivates the resilience and strength that will eventually break through into the light.

## The Tapestry of Life

The psalmist declares, "Even the darkness will not be dark to you; the night will shine like the day, for darkness is as light to you." This powerful reassurance reminds us that there's no place too dark for God's light to penetrate. His presence in the darkness brings hope, comfort, and guidance. We are never truly alone; His light is always with us, illuminating our path, even when it feels obscured by shadows.

Consider the story of Joseph in the book of Genesis. His journey took him through the darkness of betrayal, slavery, and imprisonment. Each of these trials could have been enough to crush his spirit, yet it was in those very shadows that God was shaping Joseph for his ultimate purpose—a position of influence and leadership. What seemed like a series of unfortunate events was, in reality, part of God's grand design. Through every trial, God was preparing Joseph to fulfill a destiny that would save many lives.

Similarly, our seasons of darkness might not make sense in the moment. The pain and confusion can feel overwhelming, yet God is weaving a tapestry of purpose through them. It's in the valleys of life that our faith is refined, our character strengthened, and our reliance on God deepened. These are the moments that shape us, molding us into the people we are meant to be.

When darkness envelops your path, remember that God's sovereignty transcends the night. He works in the hidden places, shaping circumstances for our good and His glory.

# A Fresh Thought from God

Each person represents a unique reflection of divine creation, a singular thought brought into existence by the Person of God. Imagine the vastness of God's creativity—a boundless expanse where each individual is a distinct idea, carefully crafted and nurtured into existence. In the tapestry of humanity, no two thoughts, no two souls, are identical.

Each person is a fresh thought from God.

It speaks to the infinite depth of divine imagination, where every individual is designed with purpose, possessing a blend of talents, dreams, and experiences that shape their distinctiveness. Just as no two snowflakes are alike, no two individuals share the exact combination of qualities, aspirations, and perspectives. This divine artistry is evident in the myriad ways we express love, compassion, creativity, and resilience. Each person's life is a testament to God's boundless ingenuity and love. Imagine standing before a vast field of wildflowers, each bloom a different shape, color, and size, swaying gently in the breeze. This vibrant display of diversity mirrors the human experience. Each flower contributes to the beauty of the whole, just as each person adds to the richness of humanity. The uniqueness of every individual should be celebrated and cherished, as it is a reflection of God's boundless creativity and love.

Recognizing that each person is a fresh thought from God holds profound implications for how we interact with one another. It calls

## The Tapestry of Life

for empathy, kindness, understanding, and appreciation. It encourages us to approach one another with reverence, acknowledging the imprint of God's own being within each individual. It urges us to create spaces where diverse thoughts and ideas can flourish, fostering an environment where everyone's uniqueness is valued and respected.

Moreover, this perspective invites introspection. It prompts us to appreciate our own uniqueness and divine purpose, encouraging us to explore our individuality without comparison or judgment. Understanding that we are each a fresh thought from God can inspire us to live authentically, embracing our strengths and weaknesses as integral parts of our personal journey.

Think about the times you've felt overshadowed or unimportant. Remember that your existence is a testament to God's creativity. You are not a mistake or an afterthought. You are a deliberate and cherished creation. Embracing this truth allows us to live more fully, free from the burden of comparison. It frees us to appreciate our unique path and to celebrate the unique paths of others.

When we recognize the divine spark within each person, our interactions are transformed. We begin to see the inherent worth and dignity in every individual. This understanding fosters a culture of respect and kindness, where people feel valued for who they are. It challenges us to listen more intently, to act with greater compassion, and to create inclusive communities that reflect God's love for all creation.

Ultimately, the concept of each person being a fresh thought from God is a testament to the divine love and creativity that underpins our existence. It's an affirmation of our intrinsic worth and a call to cherish the beauty found in the kaleidoscope of humanity.

As we embrace the truth that each person is a fresh thought from God, let us walk in gratitude for the diversity that enriches our lives and brings us closer to the image of God reflected in every individual. Each person is to be treasured, valued, and loved just as our Creator loves us. Let us honor this divine creativity by celebrating the differences that make us unique, recognizing the beauty in every soul we encounter, and living in a way that reflects the love and respect we have received from God.

# The Apprenticeship of Adversity

Adversity, though often unwelcome, is a profound teacher in life's grand tapestry. In its unwavering presence, it offers lessons that no textbook or classroom could impart. Like a master craftsman shaping raw material into a masterpiece, adversity molds and refines the very essence of our being, chiseling away at our rough edges and revealing the core of who we are meant to be. The apprenticeship of adversity begins with resistance. We feel the weight of its challenge, pushing us down, testing our limits, and often leaving us gasping for breath. This struggle is not gentle; it is a fierce battle that demands every ounce of our strength and willpower. Yet, within this relentless struggle lies the seed of transformation. Adversity, in its demanding tutelage, beckons us to embrace resilience and adaptability. It compels us to dig deep within ourselves to find the fortitude to persevere. Each trial, each obstacle, becomes a steppingstone, teaching us the invaluable art of endurance and the beauty of rising again after each fall.

In the crucible of adversity, we discover the depths of our own courage. It is in the darkest moments, when the weight of the world seems unbearable, that our true strength is revealed. Adversity pushes us beyond our perceived limits, urging us to confront our deepest fears and doubts. It strips away our pretenses and forces us to face our vulnerabilities head-on. This crucible becomes the forge where our character is tempered, revealing an inner resilience we never knew existed. We learn that courage is not the absence of fear but the determination to move forward despite it.

Moreover, this apprenticeship unveils empathy within us. As we navigate our own adversities, we gain a deeper understanding of the struggles of others. Each pain we endure, each challenge we overcome, softens our hearts and opens our eyes to the suffering around us. We begin to see the world through the lens of shared humanity, realizing that we are not alone in our struggles. This newfound empathy enables us to extend compassion and support to our fellow travelers, offering a listening ear, a comforting word, and a helping hand to those in need.

Adversity doesn't discriminate; it visits each life with its unique trials. It comes to us all, regardless of our status, background, or circumstances. Yet, in its impartiality lies a profound lesson—that growth springs forth from adversity's touch. It is an opportunity for us to refine our perspectives, to cultivate gratitude amidst hardship, and to glean wisdom from the most challenging chapters of our lives. We learn to appreciate the small victories, to find beauty in the midst of pain, and to recognize the strength that lies within us.

Therefore, let us approach the apprenticeship of adversity with an open heart and a teachable spirit. Embrace its lessons, for within its formidable grasp lies the transformative power to shape us into resilient, empathetic beings. We become individuals capable of weathering life's storms and emerging as stronger, wiser souls. Each trial we face, each hardship we endure, becomes a testament to our inner strength and a beacon of hope for others. Adversity, though often unwelcome, becomes a powerful teacher, guiding us on a journey of self-discovery and growth. Let us welcome its lessons, knowing that through adversity, we are molded into the best versions of ourselves.

# The Fingerprints of God

In the quiet moments of life, when the world seems to hush its bustling rhythm, we have the profound opportunity to ponder the intricate fingerprints of God. These fingerprints are not merely physical impressions on creation, but also profound metaphors for His unique and personal touch upon our lives.

Much like the grooves and lines on our fingertips, God's presence is distinct in each of us, marking us with individuality and purpose. His fingerprints adorn every aspect of our existence, shaping our personalities, guiding our paths, and instilling within us the beauty of diversity. Each line, each curve on our hands, is a testament to His intimate involvement in our lives, a reminder that we are wonderfully and fearfully made.

Consider the wonders of nature: the delicate patterns on a butterfly's wing, the intricate design of a snowflake, or the vibrant hues of a sunset. Each of these details is a whisper of God's artistry. In these minute and marvelous designs, we witness the profound creativity of His touch, each stroke reflecting His boundless imagination and attention to beauty. The way a leaf unfurls, the way a river carves its path through the landscape, the way stars twinkle in the vast expanse of the night sky—all are evidence of His detailed handiwork.

Yet, the fingerprints of God extend far beyond the tangible world. They are woven into the very fabric of our experiences—the moments of joy that warm our hearts, the challenges that shape our character, and the serendipitous encounters that leave

# The Tapestry of Life

indelible imprints on our souls. Each joy, each sorrow, each unexpected blessing, carries the mark of His divine orchestration.

When we encounter love in its purest form, feel the gentle whisper of peace amidst chaos, or experience the warmth of compassion from another, we are touching the undeniable presence of God's fingerprints. These are moments that transcend the ordinary, moments where heaven touches earth, and we are reminded of the divine presence that permeates our lives. The comforting embrace of a friend, the serene quiet of a sunrise, the stirring notes of a beautiful melody—these are all echoes of God's loving touch.

But perhaps most awe-inspiring is the way God's fingerprints intertwine within us, guiding us through the maze of life. In moments of uncertainty, when we feel lost or alone, His touch remains, a constant reminder that we are never forsaken. His fingerprints are there in our moments of triumph and in our deepest valleys, a steadfast presence guiding us, comforting us, and reminding us that we are never alone. They are in the quiet promptings of our conscience, in the surge of courage that propels us forward, and in the peace that surpasses all understanding.

In seeking God's fingerprints, we are invited into a deeper relationship with Him. It's an invitation to marvel at His handiwork, to embrace the uniqueness He has placed within us, and to recognize that every detail of our existence reflects His loving craftsmanship. It is a call to open our eyes to the wonder all around us, to see His hand in the ordinary and the extraordinary, to appreciate the beauty He has woven into every facet of our lives.

May we pause amidst the rush of life to behold the fingerprints of God, acknowledging His presence in the grand tapestry of creation and within the intricacies of our own lives. For in those moments of recognition, we find a profound sense of belonging—a reassurance that we are cherished and known by the One whose fingerprints grace our very being. Let us take time to notice the divine artistry in the world around us and within us, and in doing so, may we find peace, purpose, and a deeper connection to the Creator who lovingly marked us with His touch.

# Seasons of Waiting

Waiting is often seen as a period of uncertainty, a space between where we are and where we desire to be. It's in these moments of anticipation that patience is tested, and faith is forged. Waiting, despite its challenges, carries profound lessons for our spiritual journey.

Waiting teaches us the value of trust. In a fast-paced world that demands immediate results, waiting compels us to relinquish our need for control and place our trust in our sovereign God. It's an opportunity to surrender our timelines and expectations, knowing that the plans of our Creator unfold in their perfect time and manner.

Moreover, waiting cultivates perseverance. It's a refining fire that strengthens our resolve, nurturing resilience and endurance. The endurance built during waiting seasons equips us to withstand life's storms and uncertainties, shaping us into individuals capable of facing challenges with unwavering determination.

During periods of waiting, self-reflection becomes a companion. It allows us to assess our desires, motivations, and goals. It prompts us to reevaluate priorities and align ourselves with deeper values, fostering personal growth and a clearer sense of purpose.

Additionally, waiting is not merely about the destination but the journey itself. It's a time for preparation, learning, and transformation. Embrace the waiting season as an opportunity for learning new skills, gaining wisdom, and refining character—ultimately, becoming better equipped for the blessings that lie ahead.

In the Bible, numerous figures experienced waiting periods: Abraham, Moses, and David, among others. Their stories demonstrate that waiting is an integral part of the faith journey. They endured trials, persevered through uncertainty, and emerged stronger, ultimately witnessing the fulfillment of God's promises in their lives.

So, as we navigate our seasons of waiting, let us embrace the process. Let patience be our companion, trust be our anchor, and growth be our goal. For in the waiting, God is at work—shaping us, molding us, and preparing us for what lies ahead.

# The Expanse of God's Grace

Grace, the unmerited favor and boundless love of God, extends far beyond the limits of human comprehension. It's an ocean without shores, a sky without borders—a profound, limitless expanse that defies our understanding. In our finite minds, we often struggle to grasp the magnitude of God's grace, for it transcends every boundary, overcoming all limitations. It is an unfathomable gift, encompassing the entirety of creation and embracing each soul with its infinite depth.

Imagine standing at the edge of an endless sea, the horizon stretching out beyond what your eyes can see. The waves of grace lap at your feet, gentle yet powerful, inviting you to wade deeper into its mysteries. This grace is not limited by our shortcomings, nor is it constrained by the barriers we erect. It flows freely, unrestricted by our understanding or deservingness. It is the very essence of God's love poured out abundantly upon us, a constant reminder of His boundless mercy.

Ephesians 2:8-9 reassures us: "For by grace you have been saved through faith. And this is not your own doing; it is the gift of God, not a result of works, so that no one may boast." This grace is a gift freely given, independent of our worthiness or actions. It's a divine expression of God's love, offered to us despite our shortcomings and failures.

In moments of imperfection, when our hearts falter and our spirits waver, it is grace that lifts us, offering forgiveness and redemption. It is the gentle whisper that reassures us that we are cherished despite our flaws, and that our worth is not defined by our mistakes. Picture a weary traveler, burdened by the weight of their journey, finding solace in a serene oasis. That oasis is grace—refreshing, renewing, and reminding us of our intrinsic value in God's eyes.

Consider the parable of the prodigal son (Luke 15:11-32), where a father's unwavering love and grace embrace his wayward child. The son squandered his inheritance yet found himself welcomed back not as a servant, but as a beloved son. This narrative vividly illustrates the boundless, forgiving nature of God's grace—a grace that doesn't wait for us to "get it right," but rushes out to meet us in our brokenness. Envision the father's arms open wide, a symbol of divine grace reaching out to us in our most vulnerable moments.

God's grace doesn't operate within the confines of human expectations. It reaches out to the outcast, the sinner, the marginalized, offering hope and reconciliation. It's a transformative force that breaks chains, heals wounds, and restores what was lost. It's like a gentle rain falling on parched land, bringing life and color where there was once only desolation.

In our darkest hours, when despair threatens to engulf us, grace shines as a beacon of hope. It transcends all boundaries, erasing the lines of judgment and condemnation. It extends to the depths of our pain, bringing healing and restoration. Imagine a light piercing through the darkness, warm and unwavering, guiding us back to the path of love and forgiveness.

Though we may feel unworthy, grace reminds us that God's love knows no limits. It is the unmerited favor that invites us into an intimate relationship with our Creator, inviting us to experience the fullness of His presence and peace. Like a tender embrace, it holds us close, soothing our fears and comforting our souls.

Our response to such immense grace is gratitude and awe. We are called to accept this gift with humility, acknowledging our need for it, and allowing it to reshape our lives. Through grace, we find the strength to forgive others, to love unconditionally, and to extend compassion without limits. Picture a ripple effect, where each act of grace we extend to others multiplies, creating waves of love and kindness in a world so desperately in need of it.

As we meditate on the expanse of God's grace, let it be an anchor for our souls. Let us revel in the magnitude of God's grace, embracing it with open hearts and grateful spirits. Let it transform us from within, empowering us to extend that same grace to others, creating ripples of compassion and kindness in a world yearning for such boundless love.

May the expanse of God's grace be our guiding light, illuminating our paths with the radiant warmth of His unending love, today and always. In every breath we take, let us be reminded of this infinite grace, carrying its essence in our hearts as we journey through life.

# The Singular Gift of a Day

Each day on this planet is a gift orchestrated by the divine hand of God. Each sunrise whispers of His faithfulness, painting the sky with vibrant hues, ushering in a fresh canvas of time for us to embrace. Our days are not mere coincidences, but intentional moments crafted by a loving Creator. In the book of Psalms, we find wisdom in the words of King David as he declares, "This is the day that the Lord has made; let us rejoice and be glad in it." (Psalm 118:24) This verse resonates as a reminder that each day, regardless of its challenges or triumphs, is a precious opportunity for gratitude and joy. It's a chance to marvel at the wonders around us, the relationships we cherish, and the lessons awaiting our discovery.

Our days are not solely defined by their length but by the depth of impact we create within them. They serve as a platform for us to extend kindness, spread love, and offer compassion. Whether it's a smile shared with a stranger, or a helping hand offered in times of need, our days hold the potential to leave lasting imprints on others' lives.

Yet, amidst the beauty of each day, there might also be moments of trials and uncertainties. It's during these times that our faith is tested, and our reliance on God's guidance becomes paramount. Even in the midst of adversity, we can find strength in the assurance that God walks alongside us, offering comfort and hope.

# The Tapestry of Life

Therefore, let us not take our days for granted. Instead, let us approach each sunrise with a heart filled with gratitude, a spirit eager to embrace the unknown, and a willingness to make each moment count. As we navigate the days gifted to us, may we seek to honor God by living purposefully, loving extravagantly, and sowing seeds of kindness wherever we go.

Remember, each day is a precious gift from God, a chance to write a new chapter in the story of our lives. Cherish it, embrace it, and live it to the fullest for His glory. Each dawn brings with it the promise of new beginnings, the opportunity to create, and the blessing of experiencing life in all its fullness. Embrace each day as a gift from above, for within it lies the potential to inspire, to love, and to be a beacon of light to those around us.

# The Pursuit of Wisdom

In the tapestry of life, wisdom is the golden thread, weaving through the fabric of our existence, guiding us through the labyrinthine paths of uncertainty. It transcends the mere accumulation of knowledge, for wisdom is the fusion of experience, understanding, and discernment. It is the light that shines brightly, illuminating our way forward in the darkness of ignorance.

In this "Age of Information," where facts and data bombard us from all sides, wisdom stands out as a beacon of truth. Unlike information, which is fleeting and often superficial, wisdom is timeless. It is the deep understanding of the world around us, the ability to see beyond the surface and grasp the deeper truths that lie beneath.

To embark on the journey of wisdom is to embark on a lifelong quest for truth and understanding. It is a journey marked by humility, for true wisdom comes not from thinking we know everything, but from recognizing our own limitations and being open to new ideas and perspectives.

Wisdom is not just about knowing the right answer; it is about asking the right questions. It is about having the courage to challenge conventional wisdom and the status quo. It is about seeing the world not as it is, but as it could be, and working towards making that vision a reality.

The Bible is replete with wisdom teachings, urging us to seek wisdom above all else. It tells us that wisdom is more precious than gold and more valuable than silver. It teaches us to listen more than

# The Tapestry of Life

we speak, to seek understanding rather than judgment, and to walk in the ways of wisdom rather than folly.

But wisdom is not a solitary pursuit. It is a communal endeavor, nurtured and cultivated through shared experiences and learned from those who have gone before us. It is a torch passed down from generation to generation, lighting the way for those who come after us.

Today, let us cherish and seek wisdom, for it is the key to unlocking the mysteries of the universe and the secret to a life well-lived. Let us approach each day with a spirit of curiosity and a thirst for knowledge, for in the pursuit of wisdom, we find not only understanding but also fulfillment and purpose.

# WHEN THE PATH AHEAD IS NOT CLEAR

There are seasons in life when the road before us fades into a dense fog, leaving us standing at vast stretch of obscurity, unsure of which direction to take. It's in these times that the overwhelming weight of uncertainty can settle heavily on our hearts, causing us to question our choices, our direction, and even our worth. The great unknown stretches out before us like an uncharted sea, and we are left to navigate without a map, compass, or clear skies.

In this space of ambiguity, it's easy to feel a gnawing sense of unease, a restlessness that disrupts our peace. We may wake up each morning with a heavy heart, the burden of not knowing what lies ahead pressing down on us. The days stretch out long and uncertain, each one filled with the persistent question: "What's next?" This relentless uncertainty can become a constant companion, whispering doubts and fears into the quiet moments of our lives.

It is essential to remember that even when our path is obscured, we are not walking it alone. The psalmist reminds us in Psalm 119:105, "Your word is a lamp to my feet and a light to my path." This verse doesn't promise a floodlight that illuminates miles ahead; rather, it speaks of a lamp—a small, steady light that gives us just enough illumination to take the next step. It's a reminder that faith often requires us to trust in the guidance we cannot see, relying on God to light our path one step at a time.

The feelings of uncertainty can evoke a whirlwind of emotions—fear, anxiety, frustration, and sometimes even anger. We might find ourselves wrestling with God, much like Jacob did at Peniel, grappling for a blessing, for clarity, for reassurance. It's in these raw, vulnerable moments that we must lean into our faith and trust in our good God, allowing it to anchor us when everything else seems unstable.

Consider Abraham, who left his homeland without knowing his destination, driven solely by his trust in God's promise. His journey was not marked by clarity but by faith. Each step taken in obedience, despite not seeing the full picture, brought him closer to God's purpose for his life. In the same way, our steps, however hesitant or uncertain, are significant acts of faith. They testify to our trust in a God who sees the end from the beginning, even when we cannot.

The apostle Paul faced many unknowns in his ministry. In 2 Corinthians 12:9, he shares God's assurance: "My grace is sufficient for you, for my power is made perfect in weakness." This grace is our constant, a divine strength that carries us through the fog of uncertainty. It's a reminder that our journey, no matter how unclear, is enveloped in God's unending grace and love. When the path ahead is not clear, we are invited to surrender our need for control and embrace a posture of trust.

This doesn't mean passivity or inaction but rather a deep, active faith that steps forward in obedience, trusting that God's plan is unfolding even in the midst of our confusion. It's in these interludes of surrender that we often find the deepest growth, the richest faith, and the most profound encounters with God.

As we navigate the unknown, let us hold onto the truth that God is with us, guiding us through each moment of uncertainty. Let's lean into community, seeking support and encouragement from those who can help us see the light when our own vision is clouded. Let's immerse ourselves in prayer and Scripture, allowing God's word to be the steady lamp that guides our feet.

## When the Path Ahead is Not Clear

In the end, the unknown path becomes a sacred space where faith is forged, where trust is deepened, and where God's presence is most profoundly felt. Though we may not see the way ahead, we can rest in the assurance that God walks with us, lighting our path, step by step, until we reach the clarity and peace that He promises.

# Keeping in Step with the Spirit of God

In the symphony of life, the Spirit of God orchestrates a beautiful melody, inviting us to step in rhythm with His divine guidance. Galatians 5:25 encourages us to "keep in step with the Spirit." This invitation is not merely a gentle suggestion but a profound call to align our thoughts, actions, and desires with His perfect will. It beckons us to participate in a divine dance, where every step taken in harmony with the Spirit creates a tapestry of grace, beauty, and purpose.

Walking in step with the Spirit begins with surrender—an intentional yielding of our plans and ambitions to His leading. This surrender is a daily choice, a conscious decision to invite the Spirit to direct our steps. It's not a passive act of giving up but an active embrace of His transformative power in our lives. We lay down our will, not out of resignation, but with the hope that His way is higher, His thoughts deeper, and His love more profound than anything we could imagine.

Keeping in step with the Spirit starts with attentive listening. Just as a dancer listens intently to the music, we must attune our hearts to the gentle whispers of the Holy Spirit. In the quiet moments of our souls, His voice resonates, guiding us through the labyrinth of decisions, and offering wisdom, comfort, and direction. It's in these sacred silences that we learn to recognize His presence, discern His will, and find the courage to follow where He leads.

Staying attuned to the Spirit involves nurturing a relationship through prayer, meditation on His word, and cultivating sensitivity to His gentle nudges. This journey of intimacy is not without its challenges, but it is rich with rewards. As we invest time in prayer, our hearts become more aligned with His. Through meditation on Scripture, His truths become the anchor for our souls. By cultivating sensitivity to His movements, we become adept at discerning His guidance even amidst the clamor of the world.

The Spirit's rhythm often challenges our natural inclinations. He beckons us to love when it's easier to hate, to forgive when resentment lingers, and to show kindness in a world that sometimes fosters indifference. His ways often stand in stark contrast to our instincts, calling us to a higher standard of living. Keeping in step means embracing the fruit He cultivates within us: love, joy, peace, patience, kindness, goodness, faithfulness, gentleness, and self-control. These virtues are not mere ideals but the tangible evidence of His work within us, transforming us from the inside out.

Staying in sync with the Spirit is not a guarantee of a trouble-free path. Instead, it is the assurance of His presence amid trials, a guiding light through life's uncertainties. Even in the storms, He empowers us to navigate with grace and unwavering faith. His presence becomes our refuge, His guidance our compass, and His strength our support. We learn to trust in His sovereignty, confident that He is working all things for our good and His glory.

Ultimately, keeping in step with the Spirit is a journey of transformation. As we yield, listen, and follow His lead, our lives reflect His character more deeply, drawing others to witness the beauty of His presence within us. This transformation is a testament to His power and love, a living testimony that speaks louder than words. Our lives become a symphony of His grace; each note a testament to His unending faithfulness.

In the end, to keep in step with the Spirit is to embark on a journey of profound intimacy and transformation. It is to dance to the divine rhythm that leads us closer to His heart and deeper into His love. As we walk in His ways, our lives become a beacon of hope, a reflection of His beauty, and a testimony to the world of His amazing grace.

# Goodness: A Fruit of the Spirit

Goodness, as a fruit of the Spirit found in Galatians 5:22-23, is a radiant jewel in the crown of virtues. It is a lodestar guiding us in our interactions, urging us to reflect God's character through our actions. The darkness of this world can cloud our judgment, but goodness serves as a steady light, illuminating the path towards compassion, kindness, and righteousness.

Imagine a world where goodness is the guiding principle—a place where every interaction is tinged with genuine care and where integrity is not just an aspiration but a lived reality. This vision may seem lofty, but it starts with the small, everyday choices we make. Goodness is more than a trait to be admired from afar; it is a daily commitment, a series of decisions that align our hearts with the love and purity of God.

True goodness blossoms from a heart rooted in love and integrity. It's not merely a checklist of virtuous deeds but an attitude cultivated through daily choices. It's about the small acts of kindness, the empathetic gestures, and the genuine desire to lift others. Goodness flourishes when we extend grace to those around us, offering support, encouragement, and understanding.

Picture the power of a simple smile offered to a stranger, the warmth it brings, and the connection it forges. Envision the transformative impact of a helping hand extended to someone in need, not out of obligation, but out of a sincere desire to make their burden lighter. These acts, though seemingly small, ripple outwards, creating waves of positive change in our communities.

When we embody goodness, we mirror our good God's nature within us. It is in the smile offered to a stranger, the helping hand extended to someone in need, and the words of comfort spoken to the hurting. Goodness isn't passive; it's an active force that transforms relationships and communities.

However, nurturing goodness requires intentionality. It calls for a continuous alignment of our thoughts, words, and actions with principles found in the word of God. It's an ongoing journey of self-reflection and growth, seeking to amplify the goodness within us while sowing seeds of positivity in the world.

Nurturing goodness demands that we be vigilant gardeners of our souls, constantly weeding out selfishness, bitterness, and indifference. It requires us to cultivate a spirit of generosity, not just in material terms but in our time, our attention, and our love. It calls us to be intentional in our interactions, to listen more deeply, to speak kindlier, and to act more selflessly.

In our pursuit of goodness, let us remember that it's not just about what we do, but who we are becoming. Let goodness be the compass guiding our decisions, the melody harmonizing our interactions, and the legacy we leave behind. May it radiate from a heart transformed by God, drawing others closer to the boundless goodness of our Creator.

As we strive to embody goodness, let us be mindful that it is a reflection of our Creator's boundless love and mercy. Each act of goodness, no matter how small, is a testament to the transformative power of a life lived in alignment with divine principles. It's a light that pierces through the darkest moments, a beacon of hope in a world that so desperately needs it. So, let us commit to this journey of goodness with all our hearts. Let it be the defining characteristic of our lives, a visible testament to our faith, and a powerful witness to the world. As we walk this path, may we inspire others to join us, creating a ripple effect of goodness that touches every corner of our world.

In the end, goodness is not just a fruit of the Spirit to be cultivated in isolation; it is a communal endeavor, a shared journey towards a brighter, more loving, and more compassionate world. May we each play our part with joy, dedication, and unwavering faith in the transformative power of God's goodness working through us.

# The Sacred Act of Listening

In the bustling symphony of life, the art of listening often gets overshadowed. We are taught to speak, to articulate our thoughts, and to make our voices heard. Yet, in the silence of attentive listening resides a profound act of reverence. Listening transcends merely hearing words; it involves a compassionate presence, an openness of heart and mind.

Consider the resonance of listening in our spiritual journey. Just as the stillness of a calm lake mirrors the sky above, listening reflects our receptivity to divine whispers. It is in the quiet spaces, where we relinquish the urge to speak, that we invite a deeper connection with God and with one another.

To truly listen is to offer someone your undivided presence. It's not merely hearing words but understanding the unspoken sentiments, the nuances nestled within pauses, and the emotions conveyed by subtle inflections. When we listen, we honor the speaker, acknowledging their significance and validating their existence.

Good listening fosters understanding, empathy, and healing. It breathes life into relationships, bridging gaps and building bonds. In a world fragmented by discord, listening serves as a conduit for reconciliation, weaving threads of harmony into the fabric of society.

Listening requires humility. It demands setting aside our preconceived notions, prejudices, and agendas to embrace someone else's narrative. It's an act of selflessness, where we offer the gift of undivided attention.

Yet, listening isn't confined to human interaction alone. It extends to nature's symphony—the rustling leaves, the singing birds—all beckoning us to attune our senses and absorb their silent teachings. Have you ever listened to snow falling and drifting with a winter breeze; the chorus of nature on the first warm spring evening; or the gleeful sound of a creek or stream making its way through a hollow? There is much joy and tranquility to be experienced in the world around us just by listening.

Let us cultivate the discipline of listening—not merely with our ears but with our entire being. Let us heed the quiet whispers of our souls, the unspoken longings of others, and the gentle nudges of the universe. For in the sacred act of listening, we discover profound truths, experience deeper connections, enrich the lives of those around us (and ourselves), and journey closer to the essence of our shared humanity.

# The Extraordinary Gift of Life

In the quiet hush of dawn, the world stands suspended in a single, breathtaking moment, a blank canvas awaiting the first tender brushstroke of the sun. The horizon is a gentle gradient, a masterful melding of darkness and light, where the heavens meet the earth in a delicate dance of colors. In this fleeting instance, a whisper of hope resonates through the stillness, reminding us that within each moment lies the boundless potential for transformation and renewal.

Imagine a dew-kissed flower, its petals cradling droplets that shimmer like the finest pearls in the early light. In that solitary moment, it reflects the essence of resilience, having weathered the night's chill to greet the dawn with quiet grace. This flower, standing in its quiet strength, embodies the perseverance within us all—a living testament that, even in the face of the deepest darkness, there exists the promise of a new dawn. It is a powerful symbol, reminding us that beauty and strength often emerge from the most trying circumstances.

In this suspended fragment of time, there is a whisper of clarity, urging us to release the burdens of yesterday, and relinquish the uncertainties of tomorrow. It's an invitation to embrace the present, to bask in the grace of the here and now. The past has already slipped away, like sand through our fingers, and the future remains an enigmatic dream, yet this moment, this singular slice of time, is within our grasp. It's a whispered assurance of existence, a rhythmic reminder of the transient nature of time, and a call to be fully alive in the present.

## The Tapestry of Life

Moments, like fragments of eternity, offer profound opportunities for reflection and growth. They encapsulate the essence of life—the beauty in simplicity, the power in presence. In a single moment, laughter can ring eternal, love can find its deepest expression, and wisdom can crystallize into clarity. Embracing the sanctity of these moments enables us to live with intention, appreciating the beauty woven within the fabric of time.

Life is a tapestry woven with these singular threads, each moment a stitch contributing to the grand masterpiece. Embrace each one with intention, for within the brevity of a moment lies the potential to shape the trajectory of our existence. These moments, though fleeting, are the very essence of our lives. They are the silent witnesses to our joys, our sorrows, our growth, and our transformation.

So, in the symphony of time, pause to cherish these instances—moments when joy alights like a butterfly on your shoulder, when grace unfolds like a blooming flower, when the profound meets the mundane in a dance of divine purpose. For it's in these seemingly transient fragments that we find the extraordinary, the sacred, and the divine. It is in these moments that we catch glimpses of eternity, feel the touch of the infinite, and recognize the profound beauty of existence.

We come to understand how rare, how precious, every breath we draw truly is. Life is an extraordinary gift from God, comprised of a succession of moments, each one a universe of potential, brimming with possibilities. Use them with intention and purpose. Savor the moments of quiet reflection, of deep connection, and of joyous celebration. In doing so, we honor the gift of life itself, recognizing that each moment is a sacred thread in the grand tapestry of our lives.

In the quiet hush of dawn, as the world stands suspended in that single, perfect moment, we are reminded of the boundless beauty and potential within each heartbeat, each breath, and each fleeting fragment of time. Embrace it all and live with the grace and intentionality that such a precious gift deserves.

# The Courageous Journey of Reconciliation

Reconciliation is a sacred journey—a tender pilgrimage of the soul, an opportunity to mend the tears in the fabric of our relationships, and restoring harmony where discord once lingered. It is a profound act that transcends our differences, offering a path toward healing, understanding, and peace. The journey of reconciliation is not just a destination; it is a transformative process that invites us into a deeper, more compassionate way of being.

In the tapestry of our lives, rifts and disagreements are inevitable. Conflicts arise, often leaving us wounded and wary. Yet, within the depths of these conflicts lies a hidden potential for transformation. Reconciliation isn't merely the absence of conflict; it's the courageous step toward understanding, empathy, and forgiveness. It requires the humility to acknowledge our faults, the strength to offer sincere apologies, and the willingness to seek common ground despite our differences. Reconciliation is about the courage to step into vulnerability, to confront our pain, and to reach out with a hand of peace.

At its core, reconciliation embodies the very essence of love—love that transcends grievances, love that sees beyond flaws, and love that bridges the gaps between hearts. It's a testament to the redemptive work wrought by God in our hearts, enabling us to embrace and extend compassion and grace in moments where anger and hurt once prevailed. This divine love, cultivated by the indwelling Spirit of God, transforms our perspective, allowing us to see each other through the lens of grace and forgiveness. It is a hallmark of growing spiritual maturity, reflecting the heart of God in our interactions.

The beauty of reconciliation lies not only in the restoration of relationships but also in the liberation it brings—freeing us from the burdens of resentment, anger, and division. It is a release; a letting go of the chains that bind our hearts in bitterness. This liberation allows us to move forward with renewed strength, wisdom gleaned from the trials of the past, and a commitment to fostering healthier, more authentic connections. In the act of reconciliation, we find the courage to heal old wounds, to repair what was broken, and to build anew with a foundation of trust and love.

As we navigate the intricate landscapes of our existence here on planet Earth, let us approach reconciliation with open hearts and a willingness to understand. Let us offer the gift of reconciliation, not only to others, but also to ourselves, embracing the transformative power it holds. It is in these heart-to-heart conversations, these moments of genuine connection, that we experience the richness of human connection, the resilience of the spirit, and the profound depth of love's capacity to heal. Reconciliation invites us into a dance of grace, where we learn to move in harmony with one another, guided by the gentle rhythms of compassion and forgiveness.

May God bless you as you undertake the courageous journey of reconciliation. May you find the strength to forgive, the humility to apologize, and the grace to heal. In this sacred journey, may you discover the boundless depths of love's power to transform and renew. Reconciliation is not just a single act but a continual process of choosing love over division, understanding over judgment, and peace over conflict. Embrace this journey with an open heart and let the healing power of reconciliation bring peace and wholeness to your soul.

# Peace and Patience: Sibling Fruits of the Spirit

In Galatians 5, an accounting of the fruit of the Spirit finds its residence. Among these virtues, peace and patience stand out as siblings in the family of God's characteristics that reside in each of His children. What, then, is the dynamic relationship between peace and patience?

Amid life's tumultuous moments, peace and patience intertwine as indispensable guides on our journey. Patience acts as an anchor, steadying our hearts, and granting us serenity to wait when uncertainty casts its shadow. It serves as a silent guardian, enabling us to endure with grace, and nurture a resilient spirit, even amidst life's fiercest storms.

Peace, on the other hand, offers us a tranquil harbor in the midst of life's tempests. It is the gentle assurance that, despite the chaos that may surround us, all will be well. True peace is not the absence of conflict but rather the unwavering calm within it; a state that is cultivated by patience.

Patience teaches us to temper our reactions, encouraging us to take deep breaths when frustrations mount. It guides us in the art of understanding, allowing us to empathize with others and ourselves in moments of tension. Through patience, we learn to surrender control to the ebb and flow of life, trusting that things will unfold in their own time.

In the dance between peace and patience, each nurtures the other. Patience creates an environment where peace can blossom, while peace, in turn, nurtures the soul and fosters the patience required to weather life's trials.

Developing this relationship requires practice. It calls us to embrace the beauty of each moment, to find contentment in the waiting, and to seek understanding amidst chaos. It is a journey where each step toward patience creates ripples of peace, and each moment of peace nurtures the endurance of patience.

Let us strive to weave these virtues into the fabric of our lives, recognizing that within the balance of peace and patience lies the strength to navigate the winds of change and the resilience to find tranquility within the journey. May we trust in the timing of God's will in our lives, understanding that God's clock keeps perfect time.

# The Beauty of Uncertainty

Life is a masterpiece, a tapestry woven with threads of certainty and uncertainty, creating a rich and intricate pattern that defines our existence. At times, we find ourselves standing at the crossroads of the known and the unknown, navigating the labyrinth of life, uncertain of what lies ahead. It is in these moments that we encounter a profound lesson: the beauty of embracing life's mysteries.

Uncertainty, though often unsettling, is also the fertile ground where growth takes root. Like a seed buried in the darkness of the earth, we must endure uncertainty before we can blossom into our fullest selves. It is in the face of the unknown that our faith in God becomes our guiding light, leading us through uncharted territories.

The unknown invites us to surrender our need for control and, instead, actively trust in God's plan for us. It reminds us that not everything can be understood through reason or anticipated through planning. Instead, it encourages us to embrace the rhythm and purpose of life's mysteries. It is in these moments that resilience is nurtured, character is forged, and wisdom finds its true home.

Embracing the unknown does not mean seeking immediate answers. Rather, it is about finding peace within the questions, knowing that life's uncertainties are not obstacles but opportunities for deeper understanding and greater faith.

Uncertainty teaches us not to fear the unknown, for our loving God is already there, guiding us along the way. It teaches us to be

# The Tapestry of Life

content with the present moment, rather than fearful of what the future may hold.

So, in those times when the path ahead seems shrouded in darkness, take heart. Embrace the beauty of uncertainty, trusting in God's guiding hand as you journey onward. For it is in the unknown that our Creator weaves the intricate masterpiece of our lives, crafting a story that is uniquely ours.

Life's mysteries are not meant to be unraveled but embraced. They are the threads that weave the fabric of our existence, creating a beautiful tapestry of experiences, lessons, and growth. So, let us embrace the unknown, for in its depths lies the beauty of life itself.

Together, let us navigate the uncertainties of life with courage and faith, knowing that we are never alone. For in the midst of life's mysteries, God is always there, guiding us, protecting us, and shaping us into the masterpiece He intended us to be.

As we journey through life, let us remember that uncertainty is not a sign of weakness but of strength. It is a reminder that we are constantly evolving, growing, and becoming more than we ever thought possible. So, let us embrace the unknown with open arms, for it is in the midst of uncertainty that we truly discover who we are and what we are capable of achieving.

Life's uncertainties are not meant to be feared but embraced. They are the threads that weave the fabric of our existence, creating a tapestry of beauty, resilience, and faith. So, let us embrace the unknown, for it is in the midst of uncertainty that we find the true meaning of life.

# Gratitude in the Midst of Suffering

When suffering overshadows our days, gratitude becomes an act of defiance against despair. It's not about denying our struggles but choosing to see beyond them. In moments of agony, acknowledging the simplest blessings can be a ray of hope—a kind word, a gentle touch, or a sunrise peeking through the clouds. We must fight for joy, pursue hope, and exist in the certain knowledge that God loves us and is loving us through our pain and fear.

Gratitude doesn't erase pain; it reframes our perspective. It redirects our focus from what is lost to what remains. It's a humble acknowledgment that, amidst turmoil, there are still reasons to cherish life and experience grace. It is in those moments of profound loss that gratitude often shines brightest, unveiling the beauty of resilience and human compassion.

Moreover, gratitude in suffering isn't solely about finding personal comfort only; it's about being a light for others. Sharing gratitude amid trials can inspire courage in those walking similar paths. It fosters empathy, reminding us that in our vulnerability lies a shared humanity.

In the midst of suffering, gratitude may seem elusive, perhaps even impossible, yet it holds profound power. Gratitude isn't a denial of pain; it's a recognition of the goodness that coexists with hardship. It's an anchor in the storm, guiding us through the darkest moments.

## The Tapestry of Life

In times of trial, cultivating a grateful heart can be a transformative practice. It doesn't mean ignoring the pain or pretending everything is fine. Instead, it's a conscious choice to shift our focus, even momentarily, from what is lacking to what we still have. This shift in perspective can bring a sense of peace and empowerment, reminding us that we are not defined by our circumstances but by our response to them.

Gratitude also has a way of connecting us to something greater than ourselves. Whether we call it God, the universe, or simply the interconnectedness of all living beings, gratitude opens us up to the beauty and wonder of life. It reminds us that, even in our darkest moments, there is still light to be found if we are willing to look for it.

So, in the midst of suffering, let us dare to be grateful. Let us acknowledge the pain and hardship but also the blessings and moments of grace. Let us be beacons of light, shining with the transformative power of gratitude, and illuminating the path for others who may be struggling in the darkness.

In the end, gratitude is not just a feeling; it's a way of living—a choice we make every day to see the beauty in the midst of brokenness, to find hope in the face of despair, and to be a source of light and love in a world that often feels dark and cold.

In the tapestry of our lives…even when we suffer…gratitude weaves resilience, fosters empathy, and unveils unexpected beauty. It's a testament to the indomitable human spirit, reminding us that even in the depths of despair, gratitude is a glimmer of light and hope—a testament to the voice of God who whispers, "You are not alone."

# Jehoshaphat's Prayer

In 2 Chronicles 20, we find Jehoshaphat, the king of Judah, facing a formidable enemy alliance. Overwhelmed and outnumbered, he turns to God in prayer, setting a powerful example of faith and trust. His story resonates deeply, as it mirrors our own struggles when faced with seemingly insurmountable challenges.

Jehoshaphat's prayer begins with an acknowledgment of God's sovereignty and power: "O Lord, God of our fathers, are you not God in heaven? You rule over all the kingdoms of the nations. In Your hand are power and might, so that none is able to withstand You." (2 Chronicles 20:6) In these words, Jehoshaphat recognizes that God is the ultimate authority over all things, including the trials he faces. This recognition of God's supreme power is the first step in his earnest plea, reflecting a heart that knows where true help comes from. He recognizes that the battle ahead is not his but God's. This understanding demonstrates a crucial principle of prayer: acknowledging God's supremacy and our dependence on Him. When we face challenges, our first response should be to turn to God in humble recognition of His greatness, surrendering our fears and uncertainties to His capable hands.

The king then recounts God's past faithfulness to His people. He remembers how God delivered them from the hands of their enemies before, recounting the many times divine intervention turned hopeless situations into testimonies of victory. This part of the prayer highlights the importance of remembering God's faithfulness in our own lives. When we face new challenges, recalling how God has come through for us in the past can strengthen our faith and trust in Him, reminding us that the same God who was faithful yesterday will be faithful today and tomorrow.

Furthermore, Jehoshaphat's prayer is marked by humility and dependency on God. He acknowledges their own inadequacy and inability to overcome the enemy without divine intervention: "We do not know what to do, but our eyes are on you." (2 Chronicles 20:12) This posture of humility is crucial; it demonstrates a reliance on God's wisdom and guidance rather than their own strength. It is a vivid picture of surrender, where human frailty meets divine omnipotence, and in that meeting, miracles happen.

In response to Jehoshaphat's prayer, God assures him of victory and provides a strategy for defeating their enemies ("the battle belongs to the Lord"). This divine assurance comes with a profound sense of peace, as the Israelites engage in worship and praise even before the battle begins. They trust that God will deliver them and praise Him in advance for the victory. This act of faith, praising God before seeing the outcome, teaches us to pray with faith and confidence, knowing that God is able to do immeasurably more than we can ask or imagine.

Jehoshaphat's prayer in 2 Chronicles 20 teaches us valuable lessons about prayer. It shows us the importance of acknowledging God's sovereignty, remembering His faithfulness, seeking His wisdom, and praying with faith and praise. It's a template for our own prayers, especially when we feel outmatched and overwhelmed by life's battles.

When faced with difficult, impossible situations, it is easy to throw our hands up in the air and say, "Whatever!" But Jehoshaphat's story encourages us to take a different approach. Instead of surrendering to despair, we can fix our eyes upon God, remember His faithfulness and times of personal deliverance, and ask Him to do battle for us. This act of turning to God is not just about seeking help but about building a relationship of trust and dependence on Him.

What are the battles you are facing? Are they financial troubles, health issues, relationship struggles, or internal battles with doubt and fear? Whatever they are, ask God for His direct, personal intervention. And worship Him, praying that all things done might be to the praise of His glory. As we face our own battles in life, may we follow Jehoshaphat's example and turn to God in prayer, trusting in His power to deliver us. Let us remember that the same God who fought for Jehoshaphat is ready to fight for us, leading us to victory and filling our hearts with peace and confidence in His unfailing love.

# Finding Hope in the Midst of Despair

Despair has a way of creeping into our hearts when we least expect it. It begins as a subtle shadow, barely noticeable, but before we know it, it envelops us in darkness. It whispers lies of worthlessness, futility, and loneliness. The weight of despair can feel like an unyielding burden, pressing down on our souls, making it hard to breathe, hard to move, and hard to hope.

In these days of utter desolation, it can seem as though the world is stripped of color, leaving only shades of gray. The things that once brought joy now seem distant, unreachable. Friends and loved ones may try to offer comfort, but their words can feel hollow, unable to pierce the thick fog of our pain. We may find ourselves withdrawing, retreating into the cavern of our minds where the echo of despair reverberates, amplifying our sense of isolation. Yet, it is precisely in these moments of deepest despair that the seeds of hope can take root. Hope does not always come as a blinding light or a sudden epiphany. Often, it begins as a faint glimmer, a barely perceptible spark. It might be a gentle reminder of God's promises, a verse that tugs at our memory, or the tender touch of a friend who sits with us in silence, offering their presence as a balm for our wounds.

The Bible is filled with stories of individuals who faced immense despair yet found hope in God's unwavering love. One such story is that of Elijah, a prophet who, after a great victory, found himself fleeing for his life, consumed by fear and exhaustion. In his despair, he cried out to God, expressing his desire to give up, to end his life. But God met Elijah in his brokenness, not with rebuke, but with tenderness. He provided sustenance for Elijah's body and soul, sending an angel to minister to him, and remind him that he was not alone.

In our own lives, we may experience moments when despair seems to have the upper hand. The loss of a loved one, the breakdown of a relationship, the crushing weight of unmet expectations, or the lingering pain of past wounds can all contribute to a sense of hopelessness. During these times, it is crucial to remember that our feelings, while powerful, do not define the entirety of our reality. They are part of our journey, but they are not the final destination.

God's presence in our lives is a constant, even when we cannot perceive it. He is the anchor that holds us steady amidst the storms of life. When we feel adrift, it is His love that anchors us, and His promises that sustain us. The Psalms are replete with cries of despair and subsequent affirmations of trust in God's faithfulness. Psalm 34:18 reminds us that "The Lord is close to the brokenhearted and saves those who are crushed in spirit."

Finding hope in the midst of despair often involves a shift in perspective. It requires us to look beyond our immediate circumstances and fix our eyes on the eternal truths of God's Word. This is not to minimize our pain or gloss over our struggles, but to recognize that there is a greater narrative at play. We are part of a story that is being written by the Author of Life, who promises that all things will ultimately work together for our good (Romans 8:28). Hope also requires community. We are not meant to walk through the valley of despair alone. Ecclesiastes 4:9-10 tells us, "Two are better than one... If either of them falls down, one can help the other up." Reaching out for help, confiding in a trusted friend, or seeking support from a faith community can provide the encouragement and strength we need to persevere.

In the quiet moments of stillness, when despair's voice grows louder, let us turn to prayer. Let us pour out our hearts to God, holding nothing back. He is big enough to handle our doubts, our fears, and our pain. And as we lay our burdens at His feet, let us listen for His still, small voice, reminding us of His unwavering love. Hope is not always a grand, sweeping gesture. Sometimes, it is the simple act of choosing to get out of bed, to take a step forward, and to reach out a hand for help. It is the decision to trust that God's light will eventually pierce through the darkness, bringing new dawns and new mercies. In the midst of our deepest despair, may we find the courage to hold on to hope, trusting that God's love will see us through.

# Living with Chronic Pain

Living with chronic pain can be an unending journey; one where each step may seem heavier than the last. It can be a lonely journey, because pain keeps us from going places where people gather, or it is the result of a conscious choice not to burden others with one's pain. Either way, it can lead to isolation and a sense of otherness. In the midst of this struggle, finding relief might feel elusive. But within this arduous path lies an opportunity for profound resilience and spiritual growth.

As you bear the weight of relentless pain, it's natural to question why this burden has been placed upon you. Why has God permitted this adversity in your life? How does it bring glory to His name? How do we navigate this challenging terrain with grace and fortitude? The trials of chronic pain can serve as a crucible, testing the strength of your spirit. They can reveal the incredible capacity within you to endure, to persevere, and to find hope in the Person of God amidst the persistent discomfort.

Living with chronic pain is like walking through a dense fog, where the path ahead is obscured and each step feels uncertain. This fog envelops you, making it difficult to see beyond your immediate suffering. The pain becomes a constant companion, a shadow that lingers at the edge of every moment, reminding you of its presence. It whispers doubts and fears, questioning your strength and resilience.

But in the midst of this fog, there are glimmers of light. These moments of clarity come when you least expect them, offering a brief respite from the agony. It might be a kind word from a friend, a prayer whispered in the darkness, or a small victory in the battle against your pain. These moments are precious, like drops of water in a desert, sustaining you on this arduous journey.

Remember, strength doesn't always mean overcoming the pain completely; it's often found in the courage to face each day despite it. Look to the people who stand by you, offering support and understanding, for they can be a reflection of God's love and compassion in your life. Their presence is a reminder that you are not alone, even when the pain tries to convince you otherwise.

Amidst the relentless ache, there exists a unique empathy cultivated by those familiar with persistent discomfort. This empathy allows us to extend kindness and understanding to others facing their own struggles, fostering connections that transcend words. Pain often makes us feel shattered, fragmented, and broken. Yet, it's through these cracks that the light of compassion and understanding seeps in, connecting us more profoundly to those around us. It teaches patience, fortitude, and the ability to find beauty in moments of respite.

The journey with chronic pain is not just a physical battle but a spiritual one. It challenges your faith, pushing you to question God's plan and purpose. In these moments of doubt, it is essential to cling to the truths you know about God: His goodness, His faithfulness, and His love. Even when the answers to your questions are not clear, trust that He is with you, walking beside you through the fog.

It's not about asking God why but finding purpose within the struggle and your sufficiency in the presence of God with you. Your journey with chronic pain can be a testament to resilience, patience, and the enduring power of God's grace within the human spirit. In deepening your empathy for others facing similar battles, whole new opportunities of ministry emerge, fostering a spirit of compassion toward others that transcends your own pain.

In the confines of the endless, arduous pain, may you find moments of peace, strength, and an unyielding hope founded in Christ Himself. The apostle Paul spoke of a "thorn in the flesh," [KS26] a persistent affliction that kept him humble and reliant on God's grace. Like Paul, your chronic pain can be a source of strength, teaching you to lean on God, and find sufficiency in His grace.

And may this journey, despite its challenges, lead you to a place of greater understanding, empathy, spiritual growth, and unique avenues of ministry. May your pain become a testimony of God's sustaining power, a repository of hope to others who walk similar paths. In the end, it is not the absence of pain that defines you, but the strength and resilience you demonstrate in the face of it. Let your life be a testament to the power of faith, the depth of compassion, and the unyielding hope that sustains you through every trial.

# Bibliography

Barth, Karl. *The Epistle to the Romans*. Translated by Edwyn C. Hoskyns. London: Oxford University Press, 1933.

Evanescence. "My Immortal." Track 4 on *Fallen*. Wind-up Records, 2003.

Frankl, Viktor E. *Man's Search for Meaning*. Boston: Beacon Press, 2006.

Kübler-Ross, Elisabeth. *Death: The Final Stage of Growth*. Englewood Cliffs, NJ: Prentice-Hall, 1975.

Nelson, Heather Davis. *Unashamed: Healing Our Brokenness and Finding Freedom from Shame*. Wheaton, IL: Crossway, 2016.

Oliver, Mary. *Red Bird*. Boston: Beacon Press, 2008.

Schweitzer, Albert. *The Philosophy of Civilization*. Translated by C. T. Campion. New York: Macmillan, 1949.

Tillich, Paul. *The Art of Being*. New York: Random House, 1962.

Welch, Edward T. *Shame Interrupted: How God Lifts the Pain of Worthlessness and Rejection*. Greensboro, NC: New Growth Press, 2012.

Milton Keynes UK
Ingram Content Group UK Ltd.
UKHW040832071024
449371UK00007B/752